MW00423021

"Preachers seeking to proclaim the gospel will be grateful for the robust and insightful methodology that Randal E. Pelton develops to preach the 'three contexts' of biblical passages. His discussion of what he calls canonical interpretation and his manner of linking individual texts to the gospel is as imaginative as it is faithful and inspiring."

—Paul Scott Wilson
Professor of Homiletics, Emmanuel College in the University of Toronto

"If you want to make sure that you are not just preaching the Bible, but that you are preaching what the Bible actually intends, then you need to read Randy Pelton. I believe that much of the difficulty people have with the Bible derives from preaching that misrepresents what it says. Pelton's mission is to make sure that does not happen. This book will sharpen your interpretive skills both technically and practically so that the gospel can be heard with clarity and with compelling impact."

—Kenton C. Anderson
President of Northwest Baptist Seminary (Langley, BC) and author of
Preaching with Conviction, Preaching with Integrity, and *Choosing to Preach*

"*Preaching with Accuracy* offers sound methodology and practical coaching for preaching God's multifaceted Scriptures in a way that not only conveys a text's distinctive message in its near context, but also locates it in the wider tapestry of redemptive history and the complete biblical witness to Christ, the only Redeemer and Mediator between God and humanity. Pastors who long to introduce their hearers to the life-transforming power of the gospel of grace, while expounding each unique biblical passage with integrity, will do well to learn from this book."

—Dennis E. Johnson
Professor of Practical Theology, Westminster Seminary California, and author of
Him We Proclaim: Preaching Christ from All the Scriptures

"Standing on the shoulders of giants such as Robinson, Chapell, and Greidanus, Randal Pelton extends and refines their approaches to homiletics. *Preaching with Accuracy* shows us how to be solidly grounded in both the text and theology. The concept of the textbi (textual big idea), conbi (contextual big idea), and canbi (canonical big idea) is fresh and well-illustrated. Written by a pastor-scholar for pastors, *Preaching with Accuracy* will help you lift up Christ in every sermon."

—Jeffrey Arthurs
Professor of Preaching and Communication, Gordon-Conwell Theological Seminary

"I always sit up and take notice when a book appears promoting some form of text-driven preaching. Pelton's book is an interesting blend of insights on preaching methodology from Haddon Robinson, Brian Chapell, and Tim Keller. It is one of the most preacher-friendly and practical books I've read in recent times. Here is a worthy attempt to take into account hermeneutics, genre, textual structure, and context in the process of analyzing a text and preparing a sermon that accurately conveys the text's meaning. Expositors will find excellent practical help here."

—David L. Allen
Dean of the School of Theology, Professor of Preaching, and George W. Truett Chair of Ministry, Southwestern Baptist Theological Seminary

"Both as a pastor and professor of homiletics, I am grateful for this book. Randy Pelton demonstrates that a preacher need not choose between explaining the meaning of an individual 'preachable unit' and the larger context of Scripture. With a pastor's heart but also with a homiletician's insight he skillfully takes his reader through a method of understanding and relating the big idea even when many interrelated ideas are present. With his eyes fixed on the text but his sermonic compass pointing to Christ, Randy's instructions for finding the 'Christ-centered big ideas' are sure to help any expositor who wants to be true to the authorial intent of the passage while fitting it in the redemptive framework of God's revelation in Christ."

—Hershael W. York
Victor & Louise Lester Professor of Christian Preaching,
The Southern Baptist Theological Seminary

"In *Preaching with Accuracy*, Randy Pelton hands the preaching minister two priceless tools: first, he helps us with the task of finding the Big Idea (the key preaching idea) of a passage, including how to find it amidst a host of little ideas in a passage. Second, he shows us how to move the sermon effectively from that Big Idea to a Christ-centered emphasis as we preach. In a day when many are questioning the validity of biblical exposition in the pulpit, Pelton demonstrates that expository preaching can and should be used to reach twenty-first century listeners. This book deserves a place on any preacher's bookshelf."

—Michael Duduit
Executive Editor, *Preaching* magazine, and Dean of the College of Christian Studies and Clamp Divinity School, Anderson, SC

PREACHING WITH
Accuracy

Finding Christ-Centered Big Ideas
for Biblical Preaching

RANDAL E. PELTON

Kregel
Ministry

Preaching with Accuracy: Finding Christ-Centered Big Ideas for Biblical Preaching
© 2014 by Randal E. Pelton

Published by Kregel Publications, a division of Kregel, Inc., 2450 Oak Industrial Dr. NE, Grand Rapids, MI 49505-6020.

All rights reserved. No part of this book may be reproduced, stored in a retrieval system, or transmitted in any form or by any means—electronic, mechanical, photocopy, recording, or otherwise—without written permission of the publisher, except for brief quotations in printed reviews.

All Scripture quotations, unless otherwise indicated, are from The Holy Bible, English Standard Version® (ESV®), copyright © 2001 by Crossway, a publishing ministry of Good News Publishers. Used by permission. All rights reserved.

Library of Congress Cataloging-in-Publication Data
Pelton, Randal E.
    Preaching with greater accuracy : finding Christ-centered big ideas for biblical preaching / Randal E. Pelton, KregelMinistry.
        pages cm
    Includes bibliographical references.
    1. Preaching. I. Title.
    BV4211.3.P45 2014
    251—dc23

                                                    2014009282

ISBN 978-0-8254-4328-2

Printed in the United States of America
14 15 16 17 18 / 5 4 3 2 1

To Michele Lynette Pelton,
sweetest southern bell,
Spirit-sensitive woman,
and faithful spouse
with me on The Way

CONTENTS

ACKNOWLEDGMENTS

Thank you for being interested enough in me to read this page. One of the most enjoyable parts of writing a book is being able to acknowledge the significant part people have played in the project. Crediting them is like writing a brief, autobiography:

- My parents, Ross and Pauline Pelton, and my aunt, Sandra Curtis, prophetically nicknamed me, Professor Randal, at an early age.
- Pastor Prosser of Weeks Mills Baptist Church urged me to develop my mind and heart at Dallas Theological Seminary where Drs. John Reed and Timothy Warren gave me a love for preaching and homiletics.
- Dr. Neil Holliker, Academic Dean at what was known as Washington Bible College/Capital Bible Seminary, gave me my first opportunity to teach Homiletics.
- Mentor, Rev. Robert McNutt, and the leadership of The People's Church in Somerville, NB, Canada in the early '90's encouraged and supported my ongoing studies. It is impossible for me to measure Bob's influence in my ministry.
- Professor, Dr. Haddon Robinson, invited me to spend a semester with him at Gordon-Conwell Theological Seminary where I could continue to teach and refine my method of

finding the Big Idea. On page 27 of his book, *On Writing*, Stephen King stated, "Imitation preceded creation." That aptly describes how my method came about. Haddon also graciously read and interacted with my first draft.

- Around that same time, Dr. Gordon Hugenberger agreed to meet with me one afternoon to teach me how to keep one foot in the scholars' world while pastoring a local church. Not a week goes by when I don't put into practice his advice.

- Founders of EHS, Drs. Scott Gibson and the late Keith Willhite, provided an environment where I could learn from gifted homileticians.

- A missionary introduced me to the preaching of Timothy Keller. Through listening to Tim's sermons in the early years of his church plant in New York City, I caught his Christ-centered interpretation and application.

- Lancaster Bible College librarian, Dr. Gerald Lincoln, has eagerly helped me throughout my writing projects. Time and time again he helps me with my research, plus teaching me the ins and outs of EndNote.

- Dr. Jeffrey Arthurs invited me to teach with him in two preaching tracks in Gordon-Conwell Theological Seminary's Doctor of Ministry program, From Study to Pulpit and Preaching the Literary Forms of the Bible. He has consistently modeled excellent scholarship, superb writing, and continues to force me to think and write more clearly. His interaction with my material resulted in an improved approach.

- Students at Lancaster Bible College Graduate School and Doctor of Ministry students at Gordon-Conwell Theological Seminary continue to test and tweak the method.

- Readers like my friends, Rik Hall and Dr. John Wise, gave valuable insights on early drafts of the manuscript. My dear wife, Michele, an excellent proofreader, detected several typos and could-be-clearer-sentences along the way.

- The faith-families and leadership of The People's Church in Somerville, NB, Canada (1991–2003) and Calvary Bible Church (2003–present) have listened to countless sermons and embraced my desire to study and teach. Without them, this book would not have been written.
- Kregel Project Manager, Shawn Vander Lugt, has been a joy to work with throughout the latter phases of this project. Shawn balanced guiding me and being open to my suggestions. Everyone I interacted with at Kregel was extremely helpful. In describing C. S. Lewis's, *The Problem of Pain*, McGrath writes, "It's faults are well known—overstatements, simplifications, and omissions" (p. 204 in *C. S. Lewis—A Life*). Careful readers will quickly identify the faults in my material and I own up to them.
- Every married author knows the value of a supportive spouse. Michele has constantly cheered me on in every one of these "extra" ministries. She is God's best gift to me.
- Finally, I acknowledge the work of my Sovereign Heavenly Father who created this entire path and graciously gives me something to contribute to hermeneutical/homiletical thinking and method. To Him be glory in the Church and in the world.

INTRODUCTION

This book presents a method for finding Christ-centered big ideas for biblical preaching, an ability that plays a major role in preaching with greater accuracy. You might recognize the titles of two, popular, homiletics textbooks in my title: Haddon Robinson's *Biblical Preaching* and Bryan Chapell's *Christ-Centered Preaching*.[1] Usually, these two approaches to preaching are not paired. This homiletical hybrid allows the selected passage of Scripture to control meaning, while also honoring Jesus' understanding of the unity of the Bible.[2] The method requires two skills.

---

1   Haddon W. Robinson, *Biblical Preaching: The Development and Delivery of Expository Messages*, 2nd ed. (Grand Rapids, Mich.: Baker Academic, 2001). Bryan Chapell, *Christ-Centered Preaching: Redeeming the Expository Sermon*, 2nd ed. (Grand Rapids, Mich.: Baker Academic, 2005).
2   Cf., for instance, Luke 24:27: "And beginning with Moses and all the Prophets, he explained what was said in all the Scriptures concerning himself." You can read more detailed analysis of this method of interpretation in Randal Emery Pelton, "Creatively Moving to the Cross: Adopting the Goal While Adjusting the Method of Early Christian Preaching," *Journal of the Evangelical Homiletics Society* 12, no. 1 (2012). I am in agreement with Wilson who believes "Preachers need encouragement to shift their emphasis to preaching the gospel and away from preaching pericopes per se. Pericopes provide essential, irreplaceable windows to the gospel, and sometimes contain a fulsome expression of it, but rarely fully embody it themselves if treated in isolation from the rest of the biblical story." See Paul Scott Wilson, *Preaching and Homiletical Theory*, Preaching and Its Partners (St. Louis, Mo.: Chalice Press, 2004), 157.

The first skill is the ability to identify the dominant meaning of a preaching portion. Here's where many of us get stuck. Many homileticians state that sermons need a unifying theme, but they do not show how to *find* those themes or big ideas.[3] The method I'm proposing attempts to provide preachers with tools to help them know where and how meaning resides in a preaching portion. This involves recognizing how genres communicate meaning.

The second skill is the ability to follow the language or concepts in a preaching portion to the gospel.[4] Having arrived at the gospel, the preacher is able to show how God-in-Christ-through-the-Spirit makes the preaching portion mean something for the Church. This method makes and maintains a vital connection between the meaning of the preaching portion and the gospel. Without this connection the preacher is not able to articulate how the preaching portion is true for Believers.

Experiences as a pastor, student, and professor led to the writing of this book. First, when I began preaching every weekend in 1991, I soon discovered that it was much easier to amass pages of notes on selected Scripture than to create a sermon. Armed with tools that training institutions gave me, I had no problem gathering pages of notes—biblical data, exegetical fragments. I had lots of notes, but no sermon; I had the jig, but not the saw.

Call it what you will: I was dizzy from Osborne's hermeneutical spiral,[5] accidentally fell off Stott's bridge,[6] or drowned in

3   Robinson, *Biblical Preaching: The Development and Delivery of Expository Messages*, 41–43. See also Chapell, *Christ-Centered Preaching: Redeeming the Expository Sermon*, 46–47.
4   I am using the term, "gospel," to describe the salvation package of Jesus living a perfect life, dying a substitutionary death for sinner, rising from the dead, ascending to the Father, and dispatching His Spirit on all who believe.
5   Grant R. Osborne, *The Hermeneutical Spiral: A Comprehensive Introduction to Biblical Interpretation* (Downers Grove, Ill.: InterVarsity Press, 1991).
6   John R. W. Stott, *Between Two Worlds: The Art of Preaching in the Twentieth Century*, 1st American ed. (Grand Rapids, Mich.: W.B. Eerdmans, 1982).

Quicke's preaching swim.[7] I would think, "I understand much about this preaching portion, but I don't know how to preach it."[8] Later I discovered that a big part of my problem was I did not understand how the genre of my Text was communicating meaning and intention (what God intended the Text to do to us readers). This was especially true for certain types of literature found in the Bible, such as Old and New Testament narratives. I was much more comfortable—not necessarily more competent—in the practical sections of the New Testament epistles.

Second, in our first residency in Dr. Haddon Robinson's Doctor of Ministry track in preaching at Gordon-Conwell Theological Seminary, guest lecturer Dr. Duane Litfin, encouraged us to "just get on the target." Our assignment was to locate the subject of a preaching portion as the first step to finding what Robinson refers to as the big idea.[9] We were missing all over the place and didn't know why. We didn't know what to look for. We didn't know how Scripture communicated its ideas. Since that moment I've been trying to figure out how to get closer to the bull's eye of meaning.

Third, I've noticed that many of the pastors I work with in my classes do not have a reliable method for finding dominant meaning in their selected preaching portions. As a result, they often focus on whatever seems most preachable. This creates the potential for sermons to major on minor concepts, which may result in distorted meaning and application. So, over the years I've been trying to help

---

7   Michael J. Quicke, *360-Degree Preaching: Hearing, Speaking, and Living the Word* (Grand Rapids, Mich.: Baker Academic, 2003).

8   Thompson laments: "In the seminary, the studies of preaching, theology, and biblical studies are compartmentalized into the domain of specialists in each area. When these subjects are treated as separate disciplines, the specialists are answerable primarily to other specialists, leaving the task of integration to the preacher, who has seen no model for integrating preaching with theological reflection." See James Thompson, *Preaching Like Paul: Homiletical Wisdom for Today*, 1st ed. (Louisville, Ky.: Westminster John Knox Press, 2001), 108.

9   Robinson, *Biblical Preaching: The Development and Delivery of Expository Messages*, 33–50.

preachers allow the biblical writers to determine what should jump out at them as they read and study Scripture for sermons.

Finally, not long after beginning to preach, a missionary friend introduced me to Timothy Keller's preaching at Redeemer Presbyterian Church in New York City. The more I listened to Tim preach, the more I began to catch his Christ-centered hermeneutic that created Christ-centered sermons.[10] It was my first exposure to how the gospel makes Scripture function for the Church. I was hooked.

Since then, I have not entered a classroom where pastors and laypeople were not eager to explore this hermeneutic. Of course, some were and are skeptical. Like me, they had experienced a kind of Christ-centered interpretation that resulted in an entirely different meaning than the preaching portion. I continue to enjoy exposing preachers and teachers of the Bible to a method of interpretation and application that preserves the meaning of a preaching portion while honoring the unity of Scripture.

In a nutshell, that's how this book came about. Here's how it unfolds.

Chapter 1 asks and answers a relevant question in a day when many pastors question the ability of expositional preaching to win the day. *Does accurate exposition work anymore?* There's no sense exploring how to preach with greater accuracy if the answer is "No." This chapter highlights 1 Corinthians 14:24–25 which demonstrates that God's Word aimed at Christians can effectively reach them and the non-Christians in church who enter and overhear our worship. One reason topical preaching enjoys popularity, especially among seeker-sensitive churches, is it is perceived to be more effective. First Corinthians 14:24–25 shows that an insider-directed message reaches both insiders and outsiders. This

---

10 Tim once told me how much Chapell's book helped him. Tim's methodology, however, is a bit more extreme than Chapell's. Near the end of this book you'll see Keller's more extreme version explained and applied.

fact keeps me from abandoning through-the-Book exposition in favor of what is perceived to be a more relevant option.[11]

Chapter 2 explores the difficulty that the presence of multiple meanings creates in preaching portions. Most preaching portions contain more than one idea. Preaching with greater accuracy requires discerning how those ideas interrelate to form meaning. All ideas in a pericope are not created equal. It is important to know whether you're preaching a big idea or little idea because this affects interpretation and application. It is especially important to consider what happens when we apply small ideas.

Chapters 3–7 present a method for finding Christ-centered big ideas for biblical preaching. Chapter 3 explores how our choice of preaching portions affect meaning and application. It's possible to choose a preaching portion without a big idea. An example is Mark 8:22–26 which records Jesus healing a blind man in two stages. The narrative is designed to illustrate the gradually clearing vision of Jesus' disciples that is portrayed before and after the miracle. Mark 8:22–26 is an illustration of an idea developed in the surrounding context. Sometimes we choose preaching portions with multiple big ideas. This is often the case when preaching in the New Testament epistles. Some paragraphs, such as Hebrews 13:1–6, contain several disconnected instructions. Attempts to merge them into one theme are unsuccessful. So, where we cut the Text for preaching affects interpretation and application.

Chapter 4 reveals how we recognize the various-sized ideas that exist in a preaching portion. The method involves discovering a

---

11 During the writing of this introduction, I was reading Barth's *Homiletics*. I was challenged and comforted to read: "The real need is not so much to get to the people as to come from Christ. Then one automatically gets to the people." Cf. Karl Barth, *Homiletics* (Louisville, Ky.: Westminster/John Knox, 1991), 53.

broad subject, narrowed subject, and complement, which combine
to form a textual big idea. This is the starting point for finding
Christ-centered big ideas. The broad subject phase is a significant expansion of Robinson's method. I present genre clues for
narrative, didactic, poetry (especially Psalms), proverbs, visions,
prophecy, and parables. There is a marked difference between the
literary styles of Genesis, Psalms, Proverbs, Malachi, Mark, Acts,
Ephesians, and Revelation. That's one reason why some sections of
Scripture are harder to preach than others.

This chapter begins to explain why some common understandings
of Scripture are not necessarily the best way to read them. An example is the way Luke 15 is often understood—focusing on the return of
the younger, prodigal brother. The genre clues for narrative—not parables—tell us that the subject of Luke 15 centers on the action of the
religious leaders who are angry with Jesus' association with sinners.
That forces the interpretation and application in the direction of the
older brother who is angry at his father's attitude toward his younger
sinner-son. At the end of the story and the sermon, the older brother
is the one that needs to come home. Anyway, you get the idea.

In chapter 5 our search for Christ-centered big ideas continues as
we move from the textual big idea (texbi) to the contextual big
idea (conbi). The contextual big idea is formed by allowing the immediate context of the preaching portion to flesh out the meaning
of the textual idea. In this chapter, I present prominent themes and
characteristics of Old Testament literature, the Gospels, and New
Testament epistles that often embellish the meaning of preaching
portions found within their literary realms.

The bizarre story of God's attempt to take Moses' life in Exodus 4:24–26 has meaning in light of God's goal to make Moses the
deliverer of God's people. Moses isn't quite ready for this assignment because he is breaking the covenant agreement concerning
circumcision. This brief narrative is part of God's faithfulness in
remembering "his covenant with Abraham, with Isaac, and with

Jacob. God saw the people of Israel—and God knew" (Ex. 2:24–25). But God also had to make sure His deliverer was righteous.

At chapter 6 our search ends as we discover the canonical big idea (canbi). Here we are exploring how the canonical center of Scripture—the gospel and its implications—completes the meaning of the preaching portion and makes it true for the Church. Some readers will recognize this as a nuanced form of redemptive-historical or Christ-centered preaching.[12]

In this chapter I display my allegiance to the hermeneutic/homiletic of Dr. Timothy Keller of Redeemer Presbyterian Church in New York City. I am especially interested in showing what's potentially missing in a sermon when I don't reach this level of meaning.

Chapter 7 concludes our discussion of finding Christ-centered big ideas for biblical preaching by showing two benefits of our discovery. Here I demonstrate how the purpose of the sermon—what the message is designed to accomplish in the lives of the hearers—flows directly out of the Christ-centered big idea. And out of that purpose come the seeds of application. A key aspect of this section explores the validity and usefulness of faith-first or cross-eyed application, urging both Christians and non-Christians to affirm their trust in what God has done in Christ by the power of His Spirit.

---

12 Chapell, *Christ-Centered Preaching: Redeeming the Expository Sermon*; Sidney Greidanus, *Preaching Christ from the Old Testament: A Contemporary Hermeneutical Method* (Grand Rapids, Mich.: W.B. Eerdmans Pub., 1999); *The Modern Preacher and the Ancient Text: Interpreting and Preaching Biblical Literature* (Grand Rapids, Mich.: Eerdmans, 1988); *Preaching Christ from Genesis: Foundations for Expository Sermons* (Grand Rapids, Mich.: William B. Eerdmans, 2007); Edmund P. Clowney, *Preaching and Biblical Theology* (Grand Rapids, Mich.: Eerdmans, 1961); *The Unfolding Mystery: Discovering Christ in the Old Testament* (Phillipsburg, N.J.: P&R, 1988). *Preaching Christ in All of Scripture* (Wheaton, Ill.: Crossway, 2003); Dennis E. Johnson, *Him We Proclaim: Preaching Christ from All the Scriptures*, 1st ed. (Phillipsburg, N.J.: P&R, 2007); Christopher J. H. Wright, *The Mission of God: Unlocking the Bible's Grand Narrative* (Downers Grove, Ill.: IVP Academic, 2006).

However, saying all that leads me to acknowledge what Fowl calls the "provisionality" of my method.[13] There is much more work to be done. I believe preaching portions have meaning, but I'm not sure I can always hit the bull's eye of the big idea. It is important to practice hermeneutical humility while suggesting a method for accurate preaching.[14] I also acknowledge that there are other valid ways of studying the Bible for sermons. What follows is not *the* way, just *a* way. Please keep this in mind whenever you're reading my interaction with the thoughts and methods of other authors. I've benefited greatly from their works. So, when I critically interact with them, I do not want to be critical of them.

Wilson puts it this way: "we necessarily recognize the limitation of any approach we take, and thereby also we remain open to other ways of reading Scripture...."[15] God knows we don't get it "right" every time, every Sunday. If we are accurate, we're only accurate to a point. Partial interpretation is something we live with each week if we're honest about the task of interpreting and applying Scripture for the Church. Thankfully, God's Spirit comes to our aid every Sunday in the teaching and learning together, all for the sake of His reputation in the Church and in the world.[16] I echo a former professor's sentiment that "nothing would make me happier than to be completely outdone by others in this task, if it would lead to greater understanding of who... God... is and what

---

13 Stephen E. Fowl, *Engaging Scripture: A Model for Theological Interpretation*, 1. publ. ed. (Oxford: Blackwell, 1998), 89.

14 For an interesting discussion that attempts to achieve a balance between hermeneutical despair (anything interpretation will do) and hermeneutical arrogance (my meaning is the only right one) see Merold Westphal, *Whose Community? Which Interpretation?*, ed. James K. A. Smith, The Church and Postmodern Culture (Grand Rapids, Mich.: Baker Academic, 2009).

15 Paul Scott Wilson, *God Sense: Reading the Bible for Preaching* (Nashville, Tenn.: Abingdon Press, 2001), 161.

16 Although the following approach does not discuss the role of the Holy Spirit, I believe He has a huge role to play in preaching. I do not want to give the impression that there is a method that eliminates our need for the Teacher to teach. I am assuming that those who implement the method will welcome the Holy Spirit's active presence in the study and during the worship service.

it means to be bound to him through the death and resurrection of his Son."[17] This is my sentiment too.

Suggestions for Pastors Using This Book

Before moving on, I want to take a moment to speak to pastors who preach and usually create sermons within a week's timeframe. I have prepared this book with you in mind. Like you, I study the Bible for a new sermon each week and, often, more than one. Sundays come quickly. If you adopt this method outlined in chapters 3–6, or parts of it, this book will help you at the front end of your study. With some practice and proficiency, you should be able to implement the method within the first few hours of sermon prep time.

Chapters 3–6 are outlined according to genre. When you begin to study your preaching portion for Sunday, I suggest you read the information in chapters 3–4 that pertains to its genre. So, if you're planning to preach a narrative in Genesis, read the information in chapters 3–4 for narrative literature. The method varies slightly as you move from genre to genre.

As you follow the instructions on studying your particular genre, you will discover the logic or flow of your preaching portion very early in your workweek. This will enable you to identify the dominant and subordinate ideas contained within your preaching portion. Within an hour or so you should have a foundation upon which to build exegetical and theological insights. As you continue your sermon preparation, you can read the sections in chapters 5–7 that pertain to your genre. This part of the method will help you move closer to sermon application. My goal is to arrive at meaning and application fairly early in the week, knowing that I will check my work as the study progresses.

---

17 Peter Enns, *Exodus*, The NIV Application Commentary (Grand Rapids, Mich.: Zondervan Publishing House, 2000), 32.

1

DOES EXPOSITION STILL WORK?

By our uncritical pursuit of relevance we have actually courted irrelevance; by our breathless chase after relevance without a matching commitment to faithfulness, we have become not only unfaithful but irrelevant; by our determined efforts to redefine ourselves in ways that are more compelling to the modern world than are faithful to Christ, we have lost not only our identity but our authority and our relevance. Our crying need is to be faithful as well as relevant [italics original].[1]

We begin our journey together with an earful from Os Guinness. The reason is because in every teaching venue—classroom, seminar, or workshop—I encounter fellow preachers who realize that topical preaching is standard fare these days. And topi-

---

1   Os Guinness, *Prophetic Untimeliness: A Challenge to the Idol of Relevance* (Grand Rapids, Mich.: Baker Books, 2003), 15.

cal preaching is prevalent because many believe it's the most effective way to reach our listeners, especially seekers. Plenty of preachers fight this nagging thought: "Maybe Bible exposition doesn't
work anymore in today's ministry context. Maybe I should get
onboard the topical teaching train."

You might not go that far. However, the success of influential,
seeker-sensitive congregations may make you wonder if exposition is
the *best* way to reach today's congregants. Many of those churches
adopted a style of preaching in order to be more effective. The choice
reflects their perception of what congregants need and want to hear.[2]

Pastor Rick Warren radically changed his preaching style when
he began his ministry in California.[3] In preparing to plant Saddleback
Community Church, Warren reviewed the messages he preached in
the previous ten years as a Southern Baptist evangelist. Using the
criteria, "Would this make sense to a totally un-churched person?"
he threw out all but two sermons.[4] Warren writes, "If I was going to
start a church by attracting hardcore pagans, it would have to be a
message to which they could relate."[5]

Warren selected topical preaching as the style that relates best to
non-Christians. His dominant approach is to locate common ground
he has with the audience and then bring instruction from God's Word
that addresses those subjects. If you're aware of Warren's ministry,
you know that this kind of preaching works.[6]

---

2   For an analysis of when the listener began to drive the direction of preaching
    see Shawn D. Radford, "The New Homiletic within Non-Christendom," *JEHS*
    5(2005). Rob Bell puts it this way: "So my understanding in communication
    is you engage people right where they are; if you don't they leave." Cf.
    "The Subversive Art," http://ctlibrary.com. 6. For a frightening look at how
    perceived irrelevance can derail a pastor, see Marvin Olasky, "'It All Fit
    Together': Interview with Bill Moyer," *World* 23, no. 5 (2009).
3   Cf. his chapter on preaching to the un-churched in Rick Warren, *The
    Purpose Driven Church* (Grand Rapids, Mich.: Zondervan Pub., 1995),
    293–306.
4   *The Purpose Driven Church* (Grand Rapids, Mich.: Zondervan Pub., 1995),
    293.
5   *The Purpose Driven Church*, 294.
6   I am aware of all kinds of voices disagreeing with Warren's methods.

So, before we get too far, there is little value in discussing how to preach with greater accuracy if pastors are losing their confidence in expository preaching. We begin, then, with the goal of bolstering our belief in accurate, theological exposition's ability to shepherd those who choose to listen to us preach.[7] To accomplish this goal I want to study a Scripture that has not received much press in homiletical discussions.

The Effective Un-Seeker-Sensitive Approach of 1 Corinthians 14:24–25

First Corinthians 14:24–25 boosted my confidence in the effectiveness of God's Word like no other Scripture. I know it's an isolated, hypothetical situation, but the Apostle Paul is wrapping up a

---

Some would say the method doesn't work, despite the results. Some say it is impossible to do what Warren is attempting to do. For instance, Lloyd-Jones asserts: "...there is no neutral point at which the Christian and the non-Christian can meet, there is no common starting point as it were." Cf. D. Martyn Lloyd-Jones, *Preaching & Preachers*, 40th Anniversary Edition ed. (Grand Rapids, Mich.: Zondervan, 2011), 60. However, I am not on a crusade against a particular style of preaching. It is not my intention to critique the rationale for creating seeker-sensitive worship services and sermons. Personally, I wrestle with the concept of creating worship services for people who cannot yet worship. All I want to do is point out that topical preaching aimed at the felt needs of non-Christians is not the only effective way to preach in church. If you're aware of Tim Keller's style of preaching, then you know seekers can be reached his way too. A side note: I did find it interesting that when Willow Creek published the disappointing results of the self-study of their congregational health, there was no analysis of how the sermon style might have contributed to this. Cf. Greg L. Hawkins and Cally Parkinson, *Reveal: Where Are You?* (Barrington, Ill.: Willow Creek Resources, 2007). Please hear me. I am only arguing that the popular method of topical preaching to felt needs is not the *only* way to be effective. I also want to be clear on this matter: no preaching style has the ability to stop carnality in its tracks. Even Jesus' teaching could not stop a Judas from jumping ship!

7   I do recognize the category of topical exposition. My purpose for this section is to help some readers reconsider the value of preaching through books of the Bible or through sections of books of the Bible. I view topical preaching as a contrast to preaching through a book.

lengthy discussion of how spiritual gifts can serve God's goals in the Church. Surely he wouldn't have mentioned this surprising and sought-after result if it couldn't happen regularly. God instructs His Church in verse 1 "...earnestly desire the spiritual gifts, especially that you may prophesy." In verses 24–25 God shows us how effective this gift can be so that all of us would desire such a gift. The verses highlight the ability of God's Word to reach insiders and outsiders with an insider-directed message.

The immediate context is a contrast between two hypothetical situations in a local church: the reaction of "outsiders or unbelievers" who enter a church service where everyone is speaking in tongues (v. 23) versus their reaction if they enter a church service where everyone is prophesying (vv. 24–25). Some suggest this visitor is "an unbeliever who has already begun to show interest in the gospel—an inquirer."[8]

So, what happens when a non-Christian visitor enters and hears the word of God? Verse 24 explains: "...he is convicted by all, he is called to account by all, the secrets of his heart are disclosed, and so, falling on his face, he will worship God and declare that God is really among you." The implication is the non-Christian does not receive a favorable verdict; he fails the examination administered by the Word of God. Bruce explains it this way: "This, he will say, is God's message for me...."[9] That's relevance; that's effectiveness.[10]

We know from 1 Corinthians 14:3–5 that the purpose of prophecy was to build up the church. Paul's hypothetical situation

---

8 Frank Gaebelein, ed. *The Expositor's Bible Commentary*, 12 vols., vol. 10 (Grand Rapids, Mich.: Zondervan Pub. House, 1976), 274. Others understand this person as "a complete newcomer." Cf. Hans Conzelmann, *1 Corinthians: A Commentary on the First Epistle to the Corinthians*, Hermeneia—a Critical and Historical Commentary on the Bible (Philadelphia: Fortress Press, 1975), 243.

9 F. F. Bruce, *1 and 2 Corinthians*, New Century Bible (London: Oliphants, 1971), 133.

10 Conzelmann believes this hypothetical reaction provides a key for understanding the meaning of prophecy: "it is not prediction of the future, but unmasking of man." Cf. Conzelmann, *1 Corinthians: A Commentary on the First Epistle to the Corinthians*, 243.

outlines what can happen to an outsider who overhears an insider-directed message. Verse 25 shows the unbeliever taking the posture of a worshiper. Bruce believes this is the production of a believer: "prophecy is a sign for Believers in the sense that it produces Believers."[11] The seeker becomes a saint during the teaching time. The prophetic Word touched a nerve.[12] 1 Corinthians 14:24–25 describes what we all want to take place in church.

A Caveat Concerning Selecting Preaching Portions

First Corinthians 14:24–25 reveals that choosing sermon topics based on felt needs of listeners is not the only way to be effective. Pastors can select preaching portions with confidence that the Word of God works.[13] Those of us lectionary-challenged preachers often select preaching portions that meet current, congregational needs. I recently completed a sermon series on Isaiah and am now preaching through Luke's Gospel.[14] I have my reasons and our El-

---

11 Bruce, *1 and 2 Corinthians*, 133.

12 It may be helpful to evaluate exposition on the basis of the phrase in 1 Cor. 14:25, "the secrets of his heart are disclosed...." As I'm developing a sermon during the week, I should ask myself whether my exposition has reached the level of disclosing the secrets of our hearts. More research needs to be done in this promising area of homiletics.

13 I am indebted to my colleague, Dr. Jeffrey Arthurs, and my friend, Dr. John Wise, for urging me to think through the rationale pastors use for choosing certain preaching portions. In his erudite dissertation, Kuruvilla explains the importance of all Scripture: "the Rule of Substantiality affirms that no part of the canon is devoid of importance or consequence; for instance, in 1 Cor. 9:9, Paul considers Deut. 25:4, a relatively unimportant [to modern/postmodern readers] Text in the OT, as being significant for the 'current' practice of the community of believers." Cf. Abraham Kuruvilla, "Text to Praxis: Hermeneutics and Homiletics in Dialogue" (University of Aberdeen, 2007), 152.

14 I guess I could be accused of committing expository snobbery. I used to think and, still do to some degree, that choosing a Scripture Text is more noble and less dangerous than choosing a topic. Recently, Barth set me straight: "Even in picking a Text the same thing may happen as in picking a theme. I may reach into the Bible, find something 'nice,' and lift it out. It is

ders concur with the decision. Usually, to break up the pace, I've chosen to preach shorter series—topical exposition—in the middle of long book studies (e.g. in between Isaiah 1–39 and 40–66) and before beginning another book study.

Criteria for selection include providing a balanced diet of Old and New Testament, narrative and epistle. There are times when the emotional and spiritual state of a congregation favors one preaching portion over another. I've often chosen Books of the Bible on the intensely spiritual reason that the congregation hasn't studied that Book yet. And there are times when I am not ready to tackle a particular Book. Pastors also choose preaching portions because of specific occasions such as holy days, weddings, and funerals.

When it comes to choosing preaching portions, audience analysis does come into play. However, I do not want to think that choosing the right topic will win the day. For instance, I know that any given subject matter in Scripture will be embraced by some more than others. In anticipation of this, you may have said something like this: "You may not need this sermon right now, but, believe me, if you live long enough, you will need it later." Both topical preaching and preaching through a Book can fall on deaf ears. Some of God's finest preachers have experienced this. The following examples, however, are usually used to urge preachers to adopt a more effective preaching style.

It's easy, at first read, to champion Paul's sermon recorded in Acts 17:22–31 as an example of how audience analysis can aid sermon effectiveness. Paul preaches in the synagogue to philosophers in Athens about Jesus and the resurrection (cf. vv. 17–18). Jesus and the resurrection were interesting to these learned listeners be-

---

dangerous even to address a specific congregational situation or experience in terms of a specific Text. In such situations we must bring the Bible as a whole to bear. Then God might perhaps legitimately speak to the situation and work a miracle. But we may not count on this. The pastor might easily become the pope of his congregation, presenting his own idea instead of God's Word." Cf. Barth, *Homiletics*, 49–50.

cause, as we're told in v. 21, everyone in town spent lots of time exploring new ideologies.

Paul begins his sermon with an attention-getting observation (cf. vv. 22–23). Then, he moves to a brief discussion of theology proper (cf. vv. 24–29). He closes with a call for repentance (cf. vv. 30–31). However, verse 32 records the less-than-stellar results of his apologetic preaching: "some mocked. But others said, 'We will hear you again about this.'" So much for the effectiveness of preaching relevant topics.[15]

Then, there's Jesus. His teaching and preaching are held up as a good model, and rightly so. Schuller explained his approach to preaching: "I want to attract [the non-Christian listener], and so I use the strategy that Jesus used. I preach the way Jesus preached."[16] What doesn't seem to get much press is the fact that Jesus was not very seeker-sensitive. At the risk of sounding like an irreverent Reverend, He wasn't always very effective.

For instance, Matthew 4:17 records one of Jesus' early sermons: "From that time Jesus began to preach, saying, 'Repent, for the kingdom of heaven is at hand.'" Not very seeker-sensitive. I am confident Jesus did not choose that topic because He thought most of His listeners felt the need for it. Jesus shows us that choosing a relevant topic is not a guarantee for converting sinners. In Matthew 19:22 the rich, young ruler selected the topic. Yet he walked away from Jesus after hearing Jesus' teaching.[17]

---

15 For over twenty years God has graciously allowed me to provide two congregations with a steady diet of through-the-Book preaching. Over these years I have experienced one main difficulty of this approach (not to mention the sheer terror of having to tackle certain Texts!): *Great sermons require great texts, and not all pastors and parishioners consider every text a great text.* More than a few times I wished the preaching portion for the following Sunday would disappear. It didn't and I preached it because of a firm belief in the authority and effectiveness of Scripture.

16 Michael Horton, "Free Space: Interviews from Our Archives," *Modern Reformation* 11, no. 1 (2002): 33.

17 Warren writes, "Anyone can be won to Christ if you discover the key to his or her heart." Cf. Warren, *The Purpose Driven Church*, 220. I'm not sure

Apparently Jesus operated on the assumption that His listeners either had the ability to receive His teaching or they didn't. He would often end His teaching with: "He who has ears, let him hear" (cf. Matt. 13:1–9). It seems no amount of audience analysis, teaching style, or relevant topics create an ability to receive truth. The real need is for supernatural hearing.

Paul frames the discussion with different language in 1 Corinthians 1:18–25 when he says, "For the word of the cross is folly to those who are perishing, but to us who are being saved it is the power of God." The description, "us who are being saved," identifies listeners for whom the gospel message is already relevant. Contrast "us" with those who are not interested in that message.[18]

If I'm not careful, I may begin to think that sermon effectiveness is the result of human effort alone. I may think that if I can simply make the right choice of topic in the study and choose the right words during the sermon, God will work. Does the Holy Spirit open the ears of contemporary listeners—both Christian and non-Christian—only when certain topics are discussed? Is the Holy Spirit handcuffed when a pastor decides to preach through a book of the Bible? Is it easier for Him to create ears that can hear with topical preaching?

Apart from the need for creating a comprehensible message, relevance and effectiveness is determined more by the Holy Spirit's activity than by human effort and evaluation (cf. Rom. 10:14; 1 Cor. 14:23–24). Lloyd-Jones warns, "…there is a very real danger of our putting our faith in our sermon rather than in the Spirit. Our faith should not be in the sermon, it should be in the Holy Spirit Himself."[19]

---

how to square this statement with those times when Jesus preached without success, success being defined as converting the listener.

18 Thompson writes, "[Paul's] task is to confront the audience with a message that it does not want to hear, leaving the response to God." Cf. James Thompson, *Preaching Like Paul: Homiletical Wisdom for Today*, 1st ed. (Louisville, Ky.: Westminster John Knox Press, 2001), 49.

19 Lloyd-Jones, *Preaching & Preachers*, 242.

I began the chapter by stating that there is no need for us to explore preaching with greater accuracy if we're not convinced that exposition still works. Through a brief study of 1 Cor. 14:24–25 I have attempted to affirm or restore confidence in the ability of Scripture to reach insiders and outsiders with an insider-directed message. Now let's move to the method.

2

BIG IDEAS OR SMALL IDEAS: WHICH MEANING WILL YOU COMMUNICATE?

Figure 2.1

Any discussion of accuracy involves locating the intended target. You've probably heard the quip: if you aim at nothing you're sure to hit it. Preaching with greater accuracy begins with identifying target meaning. Preaching portions often have multiple meanings. In this chapter, I explain how various genres communicate dominant meaning. This helps us preach big ideas instead of small ideas. The spinoff is an ability to deliberately preach smaller ideas in context.

33

Think of the ideas within preaching portions and sermons as the various sized light bulbs in Figure 2.1. The larger bulbs represent the more dominant ideas that determine meaning. The smaller light bulbs represent subordinate ideas that mean something in connection with the dominant ideas. The presence of multiple ideas in preaching portions and sermons create issues.[1]

First, the presence of multiple ideas in preaching portions presents the potential for many meanings. Are all these meanings equal? Through grammatical and syntactical structure does God highlight which meaning He wants communicated? What happens when I create a sermon that majors on a minor idea? When I assign students the task of locating the dominant idea within a preaching portion, they often complain that there are too many ideas. What they are telling me is they aren't able to differentiate between big and small ideas.

Second, the presence of multiple ideas in sermons presents the potential for congregants to hear many meanings. A common complaint about preaching is that sermons contain too many ideas. So, what happens when our listeners hear many disconnected or loosely connected ideas in a sermon? Upon which meaning do they latch? Surely, every idea within a preaching portion deserves equal sermon time, right? Wrong.

Preaching portions contain ideas that interrelate. Preaching with greater accuracy involves understanding how ideas cooperate to make meaning (see Figure 2.2). Some ideas are meaning-starters; some ideas are meaning-supporters. If we preach a big idea, we should know how the little ideas support meaning. If we decide to preach a little idea, we should know how the big idea starts the meaning supported by the little idea.

---

1   We are dealing with what is sometimes referred to as the polysemy of language. Westphal understands this to mean "that meaning is contextual, that words have different meanings in different contexts." Cf. Merold Westphal, *Whose Community? Which Interpretation? Philosophical Hermeneutics for the Church*, ed. James K. A. Smith, The Church and Postmodern Culture (Grand Rapids, Mich.: Baker Academic, 2009), 65. I am talking about the presence of multiple ideas within a given Text.

The ability to identify various sized ideas and understand their interconnectedness achieves two benefits for our listeners: (1) they hear a more accurate presentation of the meaning of a preaching portion (you've majored on a major idea instead of majoring on a minor idea); (2) they hear harmony as when multiple notes on a piano create a musical chord.

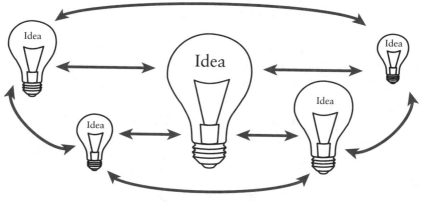

Figure 2.2

Let me illustrate from Exodus 19:4–8.

> "You yourselves have seen what I did to the
> Egyptians, and how I bore you on eagles' wings
> and brought you to myself. Now therefore, if you
> will indeed obey my voice and keep my covenant,
> you shall be my treasured possession among all
> peoples, for all the earth is mine; and you shall
> be to me a kingdom of priests and a holy nation.
> These are the words that you shall speak to the
> people of Israel." So Moses came and called the
> elders of the people and set before them all these
> words that the Lord had commanded him. All the
> people answered together and said, "All that the

LORD has spoken we will do." And Moses reported
the words of the people to the LORD.

This passage contains several ideas. One is the Lord bearing Israel on eagles' wings. Another one is keeping God's covenant. Yet
another idea is Israel being a holy nation. There are plenty more
in the paragraph. These ideas mean something by themselves and
they mean something else—something more—in conjunction with
each other in context.

If I asked you what it means that the Lord bore Israel on
eagles' wings, you might say: *God delivered them from danger
in Egypt.* If I asked you what that concept means in relation to
the other ideas in the preaching portion, then you might say that
*God's saving Israel from slavery in Egypt is what obligates Is-
rael to obey God's covenant.* Two different meanings. Only the
second idea, meaning as the collaboration of ideas, contains the
implication of God's redemption for His people. The first, smaller
idea is theology without purpose.

What about the meaning of Israel being a holy nation? As an
exegetical fragment it might mean *God's people are separated from
the other nations in that region by being dedicated to the worship
and service of God.* But Israel being a holy nation means something different in relation to other ideas in the preaching portion.
Israel being a holy nation is *one result of meeting the condition of
obedience and covenant keeping.* The meaning of Israel being a
holy nation changes in light of the context.[2] If you only communicate the first meanings stated above, they may not be sufficient for
the teaching time in church. It's not that those meanings are not
biblical, but as Wright says, they're not biblical enough.[3]

---

2   The subordination of the idea of Israel being a holy nation to the idea of
    obedience and covenant keeping is suggested by the "if you will...[then] you
    shall be" construction.
3   Christopher J. H. Wright, *The Mission of God: Unlocking the Bible's Grand
    Narrative* (Downers Grove, Ill.: IVP Academic, 2006), 277.

Idea	Idea in isolation	Ideas in conjunction with each other
The Lord bearing Israel on eagles' wings	God delivered Israel from danger in Egypt	God's saving Israel from slavery in Egypt is what obligates Israel to obey God's covenant
Israel being a holy nation	God's people are separated from the other nations in that region by being dedicated to the worship and service of God	Israel being a holy nation is one result of meeting the condition of obedience and covenant-keeping

Consider Rob Bell's take on multiple meanings within a preaching portion. "The rabbis believe that the Text is like a gem," he writes, "the more you turn it the more the light refracts. I heard a guy one time say, 'Oh yeah, I got a sermon on that verse. I got it pretty much nailed.' What? Are you out of your mind? You have that nailed? I just endlessly turn it."[4] This inevitably results in preaching little ideas.

Bell gives one example of his six-month series on John 3:16, a sermon focusing on the word "that." Bell writes, "Some Christian traditions think a Text has *a* meaning and if you apply the right method, then you can pull out the correct meaning. That's the ultimate in arrogance. If it's a living Word, then turn the gem."[5] Okay.

---

4   Rob Bell, "The Subversive Art," http://ctlibrary.com/le/2004/spring/1.24.
5   Ibid.

If you are going to turn the gem, then at least realize that you are preaching smaller ideas. At least consider that these little ideas mean one thing by themselves and another thing in relationship to the other ideas in John 3:16.

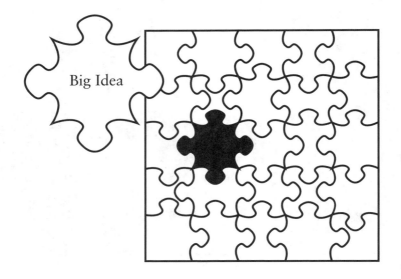

Ames begs to differ with Bell's approach: "There is only one meaning for every place in Scripture. Otherwise the meaning of Scripture would not only be unclear and uncertain, but there would be no meaning at all—for anything which does not mean one thing surely means nothing."[6] The writers of the Westminster Confession of Faith also believed in the univalence [single meaning] of Scripture when they wrote that the "full sense of every biblical text 'is not manifold, but one.'"[7]

---

6   Richard L. Pratt, *He Gave Us Stories* (Phillipsburg, N.J.: P. & R. Pub., 1993), 113.

7   Ibid. Pratt also cites the statement that appears in the Chicago Statement on Biblical Hermeneutics: "We affirm that the meaning expressed in each Biblical Text is single, definite and fixed."

So, which is right? Both the polyvalence [multiple meanings] and univalence approaches reveal the need to understand how ideas work together to form meaning. There's nothing wrong with focusing on a "that" in a preaching portion as long as you understand how *that* concept fits with other ideas in John 3:16 to create meaning.[8] When you select an idea for the focus of your sermon, be sure you're aware of the effect that other ideas have on the idea you've selected.

The "that" in John 3:16 has meaning, but not dominant meaning. It's a little idea. Preaching with greater accuracy involves knowing how big ideas and little ideas interrelate to create meanings. We run the risk of misinterpreting and misapplying preaching portions if we major on minor ideas.

Let me explain from Hebrews 1:1–4 what can happen when a sermon majors on a minor idea.

> Long ago, at many times and in many ways, God spoke to our fathers by the prophets, but in these last days he has spoken to us by his Son, whom he appointed the heir of all things, through whom also he created the world. He is the radiance of the glory of God and the exact imprint of his nature, and he upholds the universe by the word of his power. After making purification for sins, he sat down at the right hand of the Majesty on high, having become as much superior to angels as the name he has inherited is more excellent than theirs.

Hebrews 1:1–4 is freighted with Christology. However, if I fo-

---

8   Then, of course, there's the issue of how John 3:16 fits into the argument of the paragraph. Since the verse begins with, "For," John 3:16 is giving further explanation of a prior idea.

cus on the phrase, "the radiance of His glory," I may miss what
the phrase means in relation to other ideas in the paragraph. One
possible meaning for the phrase, "the radiance of His glory," is that
Jesus Christ contains the same Divine glory as God the Father.
That meaning is true to a point.

However, the Christology means something more in relation
to the idea of God speaking to us in His Son (v. 2). It is because
Jesus is the radiance of God's glory that we should make sure we
listen carefully to Him. Notice, again, that the meaning resulting
from the interrelation of ideas contains theology for the Church.
Christological information leads to application.

Let's explore possible applications of these two meanings. A
sermon focusing on Jesus being the radiance of God's glory might
urge parishioners to believe in the deity of Christ or embrace Him
as their only Savior. A sermon that communicates the deity of
Christ in relation to the idea of God speaking through His Son
will urge congregants to listen to Him. The first application is not
wrong. However, it doesn't take into account the author's reason
for including such majestic Christology.[9]

As you study a preaching portion, ask yourself which size idea
you are communicating. If you are communicating a subordinate
idea, realize that you will be explaining and applying exegetical
fragments. Those fragments are designed to mean something in
relation to a larger idea.

---

9   Fee warns, "The great danger in preaching through a biblical book, or
    in letting the Text determine the sermon, is that the sermon itself may
    become an exercise in exegesis. Such a 'sermon' is exposition without
    aim, information without focus." Cf. Gordon D. Fee, *New Testament
    Exegesis: A Handbook for Students and Pastors*, 3rd ed. (Louisville,
    Ky.: Westminster John Knox Press, 2002), 135. This danger is avoided
    when the fragments are interpreted and applied in light of the immediate
    context that contains the aim or focus for which the section is written. In
    the case of Hebrews 1:1–4, the immediate context of chapter 2:1 confirms
    our interpretation and application: "Therefore we must pay much closer
    attention to what we have heard, lest we drift away from it."

Which of the Three Big Ideas
Will You Communicate?

Preaching with greater accuracy not only involves an awareness of the different size ideas in your preaching portion. It also involves the realization that our entire preaching portion might be a smaller idea. We'll call the meaning of a preaching portion the textual big idea (texbi). There are two other options to preach.

The contextual big idea (conbi) is what our preaching portion means in relation to its immediate context. The canonical big idea (canbi) is what our preaching portion means in relation to the entire Canon of Scripture. The preaching portion means something by itself. It may mean something more, but not different, when interpreted within the context of the book of the Bible in which it is found. It may mean something even more, but not different, in relation to the Canon.

Old Testament   # New Testament

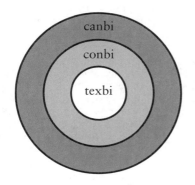
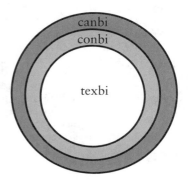

Figure 2.3

Figure 2.3 shows three concentric circles of context. The smallest circle represents our preaching portion. The next circle represents the book of the Bible from which our preaching portion comes. The out-side circle represents the entire Bible. Because of the unity of Scrip-ture and the progress of revelation from Old to New Testament, the meaning of a particular preaching portion may undergo some *expansion* when it is interpreted in light of the two, broader contexts.[10] The data from the expanded context interacts with the preaching portion and may result in modified meanings and applications.[11]

How significant is this for preaching? Very significant, de-pending on where your preaching portion sits in the Canon. Gen-erally speaking, the affect of broadening context on meaning is greater on Old Testament preaching portions than it is on New Testament ones.

For example, look at what happens to the meaning of Exodus 22:31. It reads, "You shall be consecrated to me. Therefore you shall not eat any flesh that is torn by beasts in the field; you shall throw it to the dogs."

As it stands alone (concentric circle #1), this law means: *Since God demands that His people be holy to Him, they must not eat*

---

10 I am working off the presupposition that the Bible is a unity that affects
    interpretation and application of all preaching portions. I realize that it is
    extremely difficult to integrate all of the Old Testament, for instance, into
    this unity, but I take that as my problem, not a problem with the unity of
    the Bible. I believe that, rather than suggest themes to capture Scripture's
    univocal message, it is better to suggest a plot or storyline since the Bible
    is a narrative. Goldsworthy writes: "I am also convinced that the nature
    of the unity of the Bible is the key to biblical theology and vital to biblical
    interpretation....Any kind of canonical approach presupposes a unity to
    the Bible that establishes the primary context from within which every Text
    is interpreted" Cf. Graeme Goldsworthy, *Gospel-Centred Hermeneutics*
    (Downers Grove, IL: IVP Academic, 2006), 234, 46.
11 Goldsworthy believes that biblical theology "provides the context for
    textual exegesis and the grounds for the hermeneutic application of
    any biblical Text to the contemporary believer." See *Gospel-Centred
    Hermeneutics* (Downers Grove, Ill.: IVP Academic, 2006), 257.
    Goldsworthy cites Richard Muller: "If [biblical theology] is the most
    difficult step in the process of biblical interpretation, it is also the most
    important one for the determination of the theological implications of the
    biblical message." Cf. Ibid., 261.

the flesh of any animal that was torn to pieces in the field. This level of meaning restates the law and includes the logical relationship between the first and second commandments in the verse. By itself, the commandment *means* that God's people will be separated to Him and from the nations by obeying a dietary restriction.

This law also means something in relation to the broader context of the book of Exodus (concentric circle #2). The commandment is embedded in the saga of God setting His people free from Egypt (cf. Ex. 20:1–2, the introduction to the Ten Commandments). Redeemed people obey these commandments; obedience to God's laws is how one lives the redeemed life.

However, in Ex. 19:5–6 we learn that the commandments function as a condition to be met. Ex. 19:5–6 reads, "Now therefore, if you will indeed obey my voice and keep my covenant, you shall be my treasured possession among all peoples, for all the earth is mine; and you shall be to me a kingdom of priests and a holy nation. These are the words that you shall speak to the people of Israel." When God's people obey His laws, they meet the condition of God's covenant, become His own possession among all the peoples, and function for Him as a kingdom of priests and a holy nation.

The meaning of Ex. 22:31 has evolved. When God's people refrain from eating the flesh of any animal that was torn in the field, they meet the condition of God's covenant, become His own possession among all the peoples, and function for Him as a kingdom of priests and a holy nation. The original meaning is still recognizable. The second, expanded meaning shows why obedience is important to God. But, we're not finished yet.

Meaning continues to morph as we interpret Ex. 22:31 within the context of the Bible (concentric circle #3). As we expand our context, we have to do more theological analysis.[12] We're no longer only concerned with the exegesis of Ex. 22:31. We're now concerned with how the rest of the Story, including the gospel of

---

12 We'll discuss this in detail in chapter 6.

Christ, affects the meaning of Ex. 22:31. And you know the rest of the Story.

Despite the good intentions of Ex. 19:8, we know God's people didn't obey God's laws. God anticipated this in Deut. 5:29 when He sighed, "Oh that they had such a heart as this always, to fear me and to keep all my commandments, that it might go well with them and with their descendants forever!" Jeremiah 31:31–34 and Ezekiel 36:22–27 tell of the time when God's people would receive that heart and be rendered obedient.

New Covenant texts such as Luke 22:20 and Hebrews 9:15 link Old Testament prophesies with Jesus' mission on earth. Romans 8:1–4 make it clear that, through Jesus' sacrifice, His followers fulfill the strict requirement of the Law as they walk according to the Spirit. This is God's explanation of how His people meet His condition and fulfill His purpose in the world.

What Happens to the Meaning of Exodus 22:31?

Meaning #1 (texbi): God's people will be totally separated to Him through obeying a dietary restriction.

Meaning #2 (conbi): When God's people obey the dietary restriction, they meet the conditions of God's covenant, become His own possession among all the peoples, and function for Him as a kingdom of priests and a holy nation.

Meaning #3 (canbi): As a result of faith in Christ, Spirit-controlled Christians who eat to the glory of God fulfill the requirement of the Law and function as a kingdom of priests and a holy nation.[13]

---

13 The OT does exhort us to obey God's laws and our relationship with Christ makes such obedience possible. However, dietary laws are no longer in operation for Christians according to the New Testament. Spirit-controlled living does create a distinct, Christian lifestyle (in this case eating and

The first meaning explains what it means to obey the individual commandment. The second meaning states that obedience to that individual commandment, like obedience to all God's laws, meets the condition of God's covenant. The third meaning states that the condition is met through faith in Christ and Spirit-controlled living. The specificity of the dietary restriction is lost, but the purpose for the specific law has been retained. That purpose allows this Old Testament preaching portion to function for the Church.[14]

---

drinking to the glory of God; cf. 1 Corinthians 10:31; Colossians 2:16–3:17). For a helpful discussion of interpreting and applying biblical laws for the Church, see chapter 3 in Abraham Kuruvilla, *Privilege the Text!: A Theological Hermeneutic for Preaching* (Chicago: Moody, 2013), 151–209.

14 Commenting on the way the apostles interpreted the Old Testament, Enns writes, "there must be more to Christian biblical interpretation than uncovering the original meaning of an Old Testament passage." Peter Enns, *Inspiration and Incarnation: Evangelicals and the Problem of the Old Testament* (Grand Rapids, Mich.: Baker Academic, 2005), 160. But does this amount to reading meaning *into* Exodus 22:31? Is this eisegesis, or what Vanhoozer might label impository preaching "whereby the interpreter imposes his or her own notions onto the Text"? See I. Howard Marshall, Kevin J. Vanhoozer, and Stanley E. Porter, *Beyond the Bible: Moving from Scripture to Theology*, Acadia Studies in Bible and Theology (Grand Rapids, Mich.: Baker Academic, 2004), 82. Believing in the unity of Scripture and honoring ever-expanding context may require us to rethink the nature of eisegesis. Is it eisegesis to read into a preaching portion meaning that comes from the broader context of the Canon? If I honor the canonical context, then it may be fair to say that the fleshed-out meaning is appropriate *exegesis*. In our current example, then, meanings #2 and #3 are legitimately read into Exodus 22:31.

3

CAREFULLY CUT THE TEXT

Cutting the Text describes the action of selecting your preaching portion, how much of the Bible you intend to preach for a sermon.[1] Preaching with greater accuracy involves understanding how your selection of Text affects interpretation and application. This chapter contains a brief analysis of

- why cutting the Text is important,
- an example of the vital role cutting the Text plays,
- instructions for cutting the Text in various genres,
- and concludes with two instructions that apply in any genre.

Each time you select an amount of Scripture to preach on a given Sunday, you are implying that the preaching portion is able to stand alone. You are saying to your congregants that the phrase, verse, or

---

1   Kuruvilla defines a pericope as "a portion of the biblical Text that is of manageable size for homiletical and liturgical use in an ecclesial setting." Cf. Abraham Kuruvilla, "Text to Praxis: Hermeneutics and Homiletics in Dialogue" (University of Aberdeen, 2007), 165.

verses function for the Church. So, it's critical that preaching portions possess a sufficient level of independence.[2] Your choice of preaching portion will largely determine the meaning you communicate, depending on how closely you stick to your selected Text.

For instance, your choice of preaching portion may lead you down the path of preaching a little idea.[3] This is the case if you select Matthew 18:18–20 as your preaching portion. It reads, "Truly, I say to you, whatever you bind on earth shall be bound in heaven, and whatever you loose on earth shall be loosed in heaven. Again I say to you, if two of you agree on earth about anything they ask, it will be done for them by my Father in heaven. For where two or three are gathered in my name, there am I among them."

On their own, you can understand how these verses are most often quoted in the context of a small prayer meeting. They seem to mean that God will answer the prayers of any two who are praying together about the same thing. Preaching with greater accuracy involves seeing verses 18–20 as containing small ideas that mean something in conjunction with a larger idea. If I do decide to select verses 18–20 as my preaching portion, I need to know that a larger idea in previous verses controls the meaning.

---

2   I use the word *sufficient* because we want preaching portions that contain big ideas, not little ideas. We're looking for Texts that contain big ideas apart from the immediate context. See the Matt. 18:18–20 example for a look at what I consider to be an insufficient level of independence. If you read the previous chapter, then you may recall our discussion of three contexts—Text (textbi), immediate context (conbi), and canonical context (canbi). So, as many have pointed out before, there is no such thing as the total independence of a preaching portion. All Texts are dependent upon a context. The question we explored in the previous chapter was how much those contexts affect interpretation of a preaching portion.

3   During his discussion of narrative criticism, Gunn explains how important it is to carefully select a preaching portion: "What are the boundaries of the Text I am reading? From beginnings and endings we make meaning, no less than from middles." Cf. Stephen R. Haynes and Steven L. McKenzie, eds., *To Each Its Own Meaning: An Introduction to Biblical Criticisms and Their Applications*, Rev. and expanded. ed. (Louisville, Ky.: Westminster John Knox Press, 1999), 212.

The larger idea is Jesus' instruction on how churches are to rescue faith-family members who refuse to turn from sin (cf. Matthew 18:15–17). At the end of the process the church treats the professing Christian as a Gentile and tax collector. The question arises: Who gives us the right to make this judgment call? Verses 18–20 answer that question. From a human perspective, the church's decision about the sinning, professing believer is backed by the presence of God.[4]

> [15]If your brother sins against you, go and tell him his fault, between you and him alone. If he listens to you, you have gained your brother. [16]But if he does not listen, take one or two others along with you, that every charge may be established by the evidence of two or three witnesses. [17]If he refuses to listen to them, tell it to the church. And if he refuses to listen even to the church, let him be to you as a Gentile and a tax collector. [18]Truly, I say to you, whatever you bind on earth shall be bound in heaven, and whatever you loose on earth shall be loosed in heaven. [19]Again I say to you, if two of you agree on earth about anything they ask, it will be done for them by my Father in heaven. [20]For where two or three are gathered in my name, there am I among them.

Can Matthew 18:18–20 function as a legitimate preaching portion? Yes it can. Does it possess enough independence to function for the Church? That depends on how much you allow context to determine meaning. That depends on your ability to differentiate between the meaning of exegetical fragments and the meaning of semi-complete thoughts. My take on it is that Matt. 18:18–20 does not possess enough independence to function for the Church apart from its previous context. It contains an important little idea.

---

4   Good grammarians will immediately realize that verse 20 functions as a reason why God answers the prayer of the two that agree in verse 19. Verse 20 is subordinate to the idea in verse 19, which, in turn, is subordinate to the thought of the church passing judgment on one of its attendees.

So, what happens if you decide to preach those three verses? Early in the sermon, allow everyone to hear the larger idea that is driving the entire section. Then, show the logical connection between that larger idea and the idea in verses 18–20. Once that connection is clearly stated, your preaching portion contains more meaning. It functions for the church in the way it was designed to function as dictated by the logical flow of thought—by continuing to urge Christians to rescue sinning faith-family members with full confidence of God's favor on the process.

If your preaching calendar includes preaching through books of the Bible, it is important to know how to preach little ideas. If your preaching style lends itself to thorough coverage of relatively small preaching portions, it is important to know how to preach little ideas. In these cases, you may find yourself frequently preaching mini-series.

In the case of Matthew 18, the theme of rescuing a sinner rules a large section of the chapter. You decide your sermon time on a Sunday morning does not allow adequate coverage of the section. So you divide the section into smaller, more manageable pieces. Because you are aware of how the meanings interrelate, you treat the three or four individual sermons as a mini-series dealing with the topic of rescuing sinners. Each individual sermon focuses on a slice of meaning that contributes to the whole. The little ideas do not stand alone to create meaning.

Another example is a lengthy narrative such as the Joseph story in Genesis 37–50. Unfortunately, God did not write the Bible to accommodate a forty- to forty-five-minute sermon. You could preach one sermon on the entire story. Even if you preached for a couple of hours, it would be impossible to cover all that material in detail. Or, you may decide to preach a mini-series on this section like we discussed in the Matthew 18 example.

I find it helpful to make a distinction between the biblical author's preaching portion (Genesis 37–50, let's say) and my preaching portion for Sunday's sermon (let's say, Genesis 37:1–11, the episode of Israel's favoritism and Joseph's dreams that got the whole mess started). The author's preaching portion—the complete narrative—might be too much for us to handle on a given Sunday morning. That's OK.

I will divide the narrative into manageable morsels. I will attempt to interpret and apply each preaching portion in light of how they contribute to the whole story. The mini-series will contain individual sermons that provide different aspects of God's sovereign ability to save His people in threatening circumstances.

Of course, you might select too much text. That can send you down the road to preaching more than one big idea. This happens frequently in the New Testament epistles where each paragraph can contain a big idea. You might try to preach a sermon on the Christian walk in Ephesians 4. However, there are many ideas in chapter 4 that could stand alone (cf. Ephesians 4:9–16 and its detailed information on the gifted people Jesus gives to the Church).

Directions for Identifying Preaching Portions

Begin at the Beginning

Whenever you choose to preach somewhere in the middle—in the middle of a chapter, story, or paragraph—go back to the beginning of that chapter, story, or paragraph. Then speed read to locate beginnings and endings of potential preaching portions. Or, begin at your preaching portion and read in reverse. As you backpedal, note the logical connections along the way. Try to identify the source of meaning for your preaching portion.

Pay Attention to the Structure of Your Genre

Genre can affect how you cut the Bible for sermons. The reason is that different genres convey meaning differently. For instance, narratives are structured differently than poems. The structure of a particular book may help determine how much context must be consulted in order to correctly interpret a selected preaching portion. Genre affects structure and structure affects context, which determines meaning.[5]

Here are some brief thoughts about finding preaching portions from some biblical genres.

Didactic

Didactic literature teaches through argumentation and proposition. Grammatical structure utilizes a foundation of strong, finite verbs that control meaning within paragraphs. Ideas are supported or developed by clauses and phrases joined by various connectors such as conjunctions, relative pronouns, and participles.

When seeking to identify a preaching portion in didactic literature, begin with a paragraph. We can recognize paragraphs by looking for:

1. connecting words that often signal new subject matter ("now," "concerning," "therefore," cf. Romans 3:19 "Now we know...")
2. a new idea introduced by a finite verb or a question (cf. Romans 4:9 "Is this blessing then on the circumcised...?")[6]
3. a list of commands or statements (cf. Hebrews 13:1–4; Ephesians 4:23–32).

---

5   See the following: Grant R. Osborne, *The Hermeneutical Spiral: A Comprehensive Introduction to Biblical Interpretation* (Downers Grove, Ill.: InterVarsity Press, 1991), 19–22. Robert B. Chisholm, *From Exegesis to Exposition: A Practical Guide to Using Biblical Hebrew* (Grand Rapids, Mich.: Baker Books, 1998), 189. Howard G. Hendricks and William Hendricks, *Living by the Book* (Chicago: Moody Press, 1991), 226–27.
6   In most cases, we can always argue that the "this blessing" forces us back into the previous paragraph. Therefore, I'm not saying that this question in verse 9 signals an entirely different idea. The whole point of this chapter is to help us think about how we cut the text for sermons. Do we have a big idea? Maybe we only have a little idea? Maybe we have too many ideas?

Watch for times when a new paragraph begins, but an old idea continues. The grammar and syntax make it clear that the new thought block is subordinate to the previous one. Romans 1:16–17 is a good example. Verse 16 begins, "For I am not ashamed of the gospel..." The grammar and syntax indicate that vv. 16–17 explain why Paul is eager to preach the gospel to the Believers in Rome (v. 15).

Narrative

A good place to begin looking for a preaching portion is at the beginning of stories. Changes in scenes, characters, and time often indicate that a new episode has begun. 1 Samuel 1:1 introduces a character, Elkanah. First Samuel 2:11 says, "Then Elkanah went home...."

As I mentioned earlier, be on the lookout for times when several stories work together to tell a larger one. Some of the narratives may have sufficient independence to warrant your selection for the teaching time in church. Remember that those narratives—little ideas perhaps—are connected to a larger narrative within that particular section of Scripture.

Parables

A parable is a story or analogy that communicates through the use of fictitious or hypothetical characters and situations. Parables often function as independent units. In Luke's gospel, however, parables can work in conjunction with narratives. Assume a parable stands alone, but see if it connects to a narrative. Look for the following:

1. narrator comments which introduce the parable (Luke 8:4 "And when a great crowd was gathering... he said in a parable..."; cf. the narrative setup in the famous parable of Luke 15)
2. a summarizing statement by Jesus that gives meaning to the parable (usually marking the end of the parable)

Poetry

Except for short Psalms, you can expect to experience long preaching portions in poetry. Chapter divisions in Psalms are very reliable. Longer Psalms packed with theology may require more than one sermon. Poetry sections such as 1 Samuel 2:1–10 function in conjunction with the larger, preceding narrative. When you encounter lengthy poems found in Job, long Psalms, or Song of Songs, major shifts in theme may help you cut the text.

Proverbs

Proverbs contains lengthy sections that are structured like didactic literature (cf. Proverbs 31). Proverbs 2, 3, and 8 appear to be individual units of thought. Then, of course, you'll encounter many of the typical, pithy proverbs that Proverbs is famous for.[7] In the middle are mid-sized preaching portions such as instructions to the lazy in 6:6–11. Often a change of topic indicates a new preaching portion.

Prophecy

Preaching portions in prophetic literature often take the shape of sermons. Individual sermons may begin with dates that mark the time the sermon was given (cf. Haggai 1:1 and 2:1). In many sections prophetic literature shares the characteristics of didactic literature. There will be times when prophecy includes narrative scenes, so narrative clues can help you cut the text for preaching.

Visions

Visions are among the most difficult genres to interpret, but they might be the easiest when it comes to identifying preaching por-

---

7   I acknowledge the contribution of scholars who have shown that more individual proverbs have a larger context than previously believed. See Bruce K. Waltke, *The Book of Proverbs: Chapters 1-15*, The New International Commentary on the Old Testament (Grand Rapids, Mich.: Eerdmans, 2004). See also Tremper Longman, *Proverbs*, Baker Commentary on the Old Testament Wisdom and Psalms (Grand Rapids, Mich.: Baker Academic, 2006).

tions. Most of the time the beginning and ending of a particular vision identify a valid preaching portion (cf. Revelation 4:1–11). There are times, such as in Zechariah, when the vision, plus its interpretation, combines to make a preaching portion.[8]

Two Instructions That Apply to Any Genre

Genres within a Genre
There will be times when your preaching portion contains more than one genre. You'll encounter this often in Old Testament narratives and the Gospels. Scout out movement from one genre to another: narrative to didactic, didactic to narrative, narrative to parable. Watch for the interrelationship between genres. An example of this is the interaction between narrative and parable that occurs in Luke 15's famous parable commonly referred to as The Prodigal Son. When genres work in conjunction with one another, this will often lengthen your preaching portion. But you are ready to turn one lengthy preaching portion into a two-part mini-series if needed.

Always Be Ready to Make Necessary Adjustments
I am assuming that you will select your preaching portion early in your workweek. As you begin to analyze your preaching portion, be prepared to revise your parameters. Preaching portions are se-lected by identifying thought blocks. You identify thought blocks by locating beginnings and endings of meaning. This means the process of cutting the text and doing exegesis are interdependent and happen simultaneously. Our discovery of thought blocks vali-dates our preaching portion.

So, it's possible your preaching portion doesn't possess a suf-ficient level of independence. Your initial exegesis says you have

---

8 The vision alone will not function well because the interpretation carries the theology.

subordinate or little ideas. If that's the case, you may need to adjust your preaching portion or acknowledge that you are preaching little ideas. Or, you might decide your parameters contain more than one big idea. If so, you may want to decrease your preaching portion.

4

IDENTIFYING THE TEXTUAL BIG IDEA (TEXBI)

"Methodical hermeneutics is the strict teacher who maintains order in a classroom that otherwise would degenerate into a chaos of spit-ball throwing, pea shooting, hair pulling, and name calling."[1]

We have carefully selected our preaching portion. We believe these verses possess a sufficient level of independence to instruct the church. We're ready to revise our parameters as necessary. Now, how do we determining what this selected Scripture means? How does it communicate meaning? How do we maintain order in the interpretation/application classroom?

Vanhoozer describes those who don't care:

---

1 Merold Westphal, *Whose Community? Which Interpretation? Philosophical Hermeneutics for the Church*, ed. James K. A. Smith, The Church and Postmodern Culture (Grand Rapids, Mich.: Baker Academic, 2009), 33.

> Stout, Rorty, and Fish, all pragmatists, subscribe to
> something like the following credo: "We believe in
> using texts for our own purposes, not in discovering
> their 'true' nature (they have none)." Meaning is not
> contained in a text like a nut in its shell; meaning is
> whatever it is that interests us about a text.[2]

You might shudder at this perspective, but I wonder how often sermon ideas are created with the same approach. The following method is intended to provide a foundation for creating sermons that communicate meaning that the preaching portion is interested in.

Textual Observation for Finding the Textual Big Idea (texbi)

1. Locate and write the broad subject
2. Write the narrow subject
3. Write the complement(s)
4. Write the textual big idea

1. Locate and Write the Broad Subject

Identifying the broad subject is the first step in beginning to decipher meaning. All other exegetical and theological endeavors build on this foundation. The search for the broad subject begins to reveal the relationship between the multiple meanings that reside in a preaching portion. This allows pastors to make decisions on how they will communicate the Text. It provides an opportunity to choose whether

2   Kevin J. Vanhoozer, *Is There a Meaning in This Text?: The Bible, the Reader, and the Morality of Literary Knowledge* (Grand Rapids, Mich.: Zondervan, 1998), 103.

they'll emphasize a small or larger idea. This helps us be intentional about the choices all of us make whenever we preach the Bible.

Over the years scholars have helped us understand how genres affect interpretation.[3] Each genre contains structure that drives communication. Different genres display their ideas differently. In this early stage of sermon development we're learning to observe how genres display meaning, especially dominant meaning. We accomplish this by locating the broad subject of a preaching portion.

Guidelines for Writing a Broad Subject

The broad subject is a phrase that begins to answer the question, "What is the writer talking about?"[4] It is broad in the sense that it does not tell precisely what the writer is talking about. Note the following guidelines for writing the broad subject:

---

3   Osborne wrote: "genre provides a set of rules...and allow[s] the interpreter greater precision in uncovering the author's intended meaning." Cf. Grant R. Osborne, *The Hermeneutical Spiral: A Comprehensive Introduction to Biblical Interpretation* (Downers Grove, Ill.: InterVarsity Press, 1991), 151. Chisholm warned: "Without knowing how these genres 'work' the interpreter can easily miss the message." Cf. Robert B. Chisholm, *From Exegesis to Exposition: A Practical Guide to Using Biblical Hebrew* (Grand Rapids, Mich.: Baker Books, 1998), 187. Ryken suggests that, "sometimes the correct interpretation of a unit depends on identifying the precise genre of the passage." Cf. Leland Ryken, *How to Read the Bible as Literature* (Grand Rapids, Mich.: Academie Books, 1984), 136. Vanhoozer provides a more in-depth understanding of the importance of genre studies: "The concept of genre, I suggest, describes the illocutionary act *at the level of the whole*, placing the parts within an overall unity that serves a meaningful purpose. It follows that genre is the key to interpreting communicative action.... Genre is nothing less than the 'controlling idea of the whole.'" Cf. Vanhoozer, *Is There a Meaning in This Text?: The Bible, the Reader, and the Morality of Literary Knowledge*, 341. More recently, Kuruvilla writes, "Genre, as a code governing reading, appears to be exhorting the reader: *Receive the text this way, to generate this meaning and to respond in this fashion.*" Cf. Abraham Kuruvilla, "Text to Praxis: Hermeneutics and Homiletics in Dialogue" (University of Aberdeen, 2007), 45–46.

4   If you are familiar with Haddon Robinson's, Biblical Preaching, locating the broad subject is a *prior* step to his formation of a subject. Robinson's subjects are in the form of a question. Cf. Haddon W. Robinson, *Biblical Preaching: The Development and Delivery of Expository Messages*, 2nd ed. (Grand Rapids, Mich.: Baker Academic, 2001), 41–46, 66–68.

- It is not one word. That's probably too broad.
- It is not a complete sentence. A complete sentence is a premature, complete idea. That will come later.
- It uses the –ing form of the verb (the –ing form prevents the phrase from being a complete sentence, e.g. "Asking God for help" instead of "Ask God for help").
- It includes the subject, object, or other phrases found within the early part of the preaching portion ("Paul asking God for boldness...").
- It sticks to the exact wording of your English translation.

Here are a few examples of how to word broad subjects: Romans 6:1–11 "(Christians not)[5] continuing in sin." Romans 8:1–8 "(Christians) having no condemnation." Romans 9:1–13 "Paul having great heaviness and continual sorrow."

Identifying and Utilizing Genre Clues

---

5   The parentheses indicate that I have supplied the implied addressee. Paul is addressing his Christian readers throughout the letter. The "not" is supplied because Paul's question is aimed at Christians not continuing in sin.

Now that we're aware of what a broad subject looks like, let's look at how to locate one. We begin by paying attention to clues provided by each genre. I consider the following clues to be guidelines rather than hard and fast rules.

Locating the Broad Subject in Narratives

Trace the Story Line

In his dialogue with hermeneutical theorists, Vanhoozer writes, "commentators are being unrealistic when they seek to reduce biblical narrative either to 'what it teaches' or to 'what actually happened.' A concept has one kind of precision, a metaphor has another, and a narrative has yet another."[6] But, as you know, on Sunday preachers do have to explain how a narrative preaching portion functions for the Church. In a very real sense, we do tell our congregants what the narrative teaches, despite its unique level of precision or lack of. Tracing the story line of a narrative helps us understand the level of precision it contains.

The main rule governing stories is the story rules.[7] The entire narrative—not the paragraph—forms the thought block of stories. The story line displays meanings and suggests relationships between meanings. So, we begin to tackle a narrative preaching portion by identifying the background (place, time, scenery, etc.), rising action (introduction and development of conflict[8]), climax

---

6   Vanhoozer, *Is There a Meaning in This Text?: The Bible, the Reader, and the Morality of Literary Knowledge*, 140.
7   Kuruvilla writes, "the path actually chosen by the narrator was one that would effectively project the world in front of the Text [i.e., how that story is applied] and culminate in application for the reader." Cf. Kuruvilla, "Text to Praxis: Hermeneutics and Homiletics in Dialogue," 84.
8   Wilhoit and Ryken write: "Nearly every story is built around one or more conflicts moving toward a resolution. This is simply how stories are told." Cf. Jim Wilhoit Ryken and Leland, *Effective Bible Teaching* (Grand Rapids, Mich: Baker, 1988), 213. Pratt writes, "Aristotle referred to 'the arrangement of incidents' as the plot (muthos) of a story. We will follow this definition and speak of plot as rising action, or dramatic flow,

(the moment when conflict reaches its peak and results in a major change in the situation or a point of decision in the characters), and conclusion of the matter.

Because of the way stories are told, the background and rising action will yield the subject; climax and conclusion yield the complement to that subject (more on that later).

Story Line and Narrative Clues

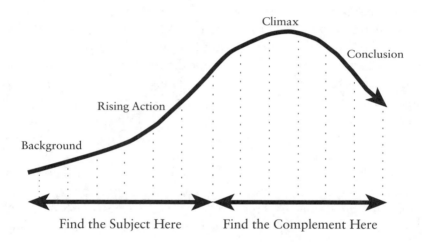

Mark 2:1–12 records the story of Jesus healing the paralytic who was dropped through the roof by his friends. I've traced the story line:

Background
When Jesus returns to Capernaum, He's greeted with a packed house of listeners (vv. 1–2).

---

as the heightening and lessening of tension through the arrangement of scenes." Cf. Richard L. Pratt, *He Gave Us Stories* (Phillipsburg, N.J.: P. & R. Pub., 1993), 179. See also Longman's helpful analysis in Moisés Silva, ed. *Foundations of Contemporary Interpretation* (Grand Rapids, Mich.: Zondervan Pub. House, 1996), 151–67.

Rising Action

Four men carrying a paralytic man discover they can't get through to Jesus because of the crowd, so they carried him up on the roof, created an opening in the roof, lowered him down to Jesus to be healed (vv. 3–4); in response to faith, Jesus declares his sin forgiven (v. 5) and is questioned by the scribes (vv. 6–7).

Climax

Jesus responds to the scribes' questions by showing and saying that He has authority on earth to forgive sins (vv. 8–11); Jesus heals the man (v 11).[9]

Conclusion

The healed man and the crowd respond to Jesus' miracle (v. 12).

Broad Subject

Jesus having the authority to forgive the paralytic's sin. You could also try: four men carrying a paralytic to Jesus for healing.[10]

Repetition of Key Words[11]

When a biblical author repeats some significant word or concept, there's a good chance he's indi-

---

9 This analysis is not an exact science. It is not always clear how to divide a narrative into these categories. The most important division is deciding where the rising action ends and climax begins. That line determines the location of subject and complement. My advice is to test a couple of options.

10 Most sermons on this narrative tend to focus on the action of the four men who brought their needy friend to Jesus for healing. Remember our discussion of the multiple meanings that exist in most preaching portions? If a sermon focuses on the activity of the four men, then the story functions as a model for evangelistic effort. A sermon that centers on the activity of the four men is going to lead in an entirely different direction than the one that focuses on Jesus' ability to forgive and heal.

11 I suggest that you utilize this and the following clues in conjunction with the story line analysis. These clues may help affirm or adjust your initial findings.

cating some facet of dominant meaning. Ryken asserts, "The most reliable guide to what a story is about is the principle of repetition. What keeps getting repeated in a story invariably becomes the central focus—the thing toward which everything points.... Generally speaking, a story will partly interpret itself by repeating that which is essential to its understanding."[12]

Words Spoken by the Main Character
Be on the lookout for the recorded speech of key characters. Those words will often become part of the subject or complement of the story's main idea. Ryken writes, "In many stories, God or, in the Gospels, Jesus makes a stated or implied comment on the meaning of the action."[13]

Key Questions Asked
By nature questions create tension by demanding an answer. Key questions and answers often direct the plot of narratives.

Let's work through a couple of examples that show how these clues function in conjunction with story line analysis to identify the broad subject.

Exodus 17:1–7:

Background:	Israel journeys from the wilderness of Sin according to the Lord's command and camps at Rephidim (v. 1a).

12 Ryken, *How to Read the Bible as Literature*, 59.
13 *How to Read the Bible as Literature*, 62.

Rising Action:	In Rephidim there is no water for God's people to drink (v. 1b); the people quarrel with Moses asking him to give them water to drink (v. 2a); Moses asks why the people are quarreling with him and testing the Lord (v. 2b); the thirsty people grumble against Moses asking him why he had brought them out of Egypt to kill them, their children, and livestock (v. 3); Moses prays asking God what he will do to this people because any more of this and they will stone him (v. 4); the Lord tells Moses to pass before the people with some elders and the staff with which he struck the Nile (v. 5).
Climax:	The Lord tells Moses that He will stand before him there on the rock of Horeb and that Moses would strike the rock and water would come out and the people would drink; and Moses did what God said in the sight of the elders of Israel (v. 6)
Conclusion:	Moses named the site Massah and Meribah because of their quarreling and testing, saying, "Is the Lord among us, or not?" (v. 7).
Broad Subject:	Israel quarreling with Moses and testing God because of their lack of water.

Repetition of key words:	Notice how the repetition of key words supports the result of the story line analysis. "Water" is mentioned four times; "drink" three times. The words, "quarrel" and "test," occur in vv. 2, 3 ("grumble"), and 7 (the two names, "Massah" and "Meribah," mean quarrel or test). These repeated terms have found their way into the broad subject.
Words spoken by main character(s):	Moses asks two questions in v. 2: "Why do you quarrel with me? Why do you test the Lord?"
Key questions asked:	Same as above.

You try it in Mark 8:27–30:

Background:	
Rising Action:	
Climax:	

Conclusion:	
Broad Subject:	
Repetition of key words:	
Words spoken by main character(s):	
Key questions asked:	

Here's how I saw it:

Background:	Jesus goes out with His disciples to the villages of Caesarea Philippi (v. 27a).
Rising Action:	Jesus asks His disciples, "Who do people say that I am?" (v. 27b); Jesus' disciples tell Him various answers (v. 28); Jesus then asked who they thought He was (v. 29a).
Climax:	Peter answers, "You are the Christ" (v. 29b).

Conclusion:	Jesus warns His disciples not to tell anyone about Him (v. 30).
Broad Subject:	Jesus asking His disciples to identify **Him** (**or you might try:** Jesus being identified by the people and His disciples).
Repetition of key words:	The phrase, "that I am," is in verse 27 and verse 29.
Words spoken by main character(s):	Jesus asks: "Who do people say that I am?" and "But who do you say that I am?"; Peter's answer, "You are the Christ."
Key questions asked:	Jesus asks two questions in verses 27–28.

Locating the Broad Subject in Didactic Literature

Paragraphs

Often, a change in genre equals a change in the way meaning is located. The move from narrative to didactic literature means a shift from story to paragraphs. In their treatment of the New Testament letters, Fee & Stuart highlight the importance of thinking about paragraphs: "We simply cannot stress enough the importance of your learning to THINK PARAGRAPHS, not just as natural units of thought, but as the absolutely necessary key to understanding the argument in the various Epistles."[14] So, while paragraphs are not technically a clue, they form the structure within which the following clues function.

---

14 Gordon D. Fee and Douglas K. Stuart, *How to Read the Bible for All Its Worth : A Guide to Understanding the Bible* (Grand Rapids, Mich.: Zondervan, 1982), 51.

Identify the Main Verb

In didactic literature meaning is conveyed through main verbs. The meaning of paragraphs is conveyed through the first main verb.[15] Since the main verb is often the first verb encountered within a paragraph, meaning often resides early in the development of a paragraph.[16] There are times, however, when the first verb encountered in a paragraph does not contribute to the meaning of a preaching portion, at least not to major meaning.

Even though occurring first in a paragraph, the following verbs should not be considered the main verbs that signal dominant meaning: beseech, beg, implore, exhort. Look for meaning in the content of the beseeching, begging, imploring, or exhorting. An example is the beginning of Ephesians 4, "I therefore, a prisoner for the Lord, urge you to walk in a manner worthy of the calling to which you have been called...." Meaning resides in the concept of walking "in a manner worthy of the calling...."

An Example from Matthew 5:17–20

Verse 17 begins, "Do not think...." Include the negative in the wording of the broad subject: (not) thinking that Jesus came to abolish the Law or the Prophets. All we've done is restate the concept of v. 17 in the form of a broad subject phrase.

---

15 Main verbs are primarily finite verbs but some exceptions exist. Romans 12:9ff. contains a list of imperatives that are participles. Be on alert for other verbals that do not function as the main verb even though they appear first in a paragraph. When you encounter a participle, it is helpful to backtrack to an earlier main verb.

16 Meaning in narrative literature is determined early, too, in the background and rising action.

You try it in Ephesians 4:1–6:

Identify the main verb:	
Broad Subject:	

Here's how I saw it:

Identify the main verb:	Walk.
Broad Subject:	Christians walking in a manner worthy of the calling.

In didactic literature the main verb is the main clue. The following two clues include main verbs embedded in questions and commands.

Locate Key Questions

There are times in didactic literature when a paragraph begins with a question that is answered in the rest of the paragraph. Matthew 11:16–19 opens with, "But to what shall I compare this generation?" The question contains the verb, compare. From this question comes the following broad subject: Jesus comparing this generation to children sitting in the market places. We're allowing the structure of the paragraph to telegraph meaning.

Give it a try in Romans 6:1–7:

Key questions(s):	
Broad Subject:	

Here's how I saw it:

Key questions(s):	"Are we to continue in sin…?" (v. 1) Note that this is not the first or last question in the paragraph. I understand the first question as introductory. It does not contain a main verb that drives the meaning of the paragraph. The questions in verse 2 ("How can we who died to sin still live in it?") and verse 3 ("Do you not know that all of us who have been baptized into Christ Jesus were baptized into his death?") help answer our key question.
Broad Subject:	Christians [not] continuing in sin. I've added the "not" in brackets to show that a negative answer is expected.

Locate Imperatives

Commands found at the beginning of paragraphs often contain dominant meaning. Other imperatives in the paragraph may stand alone or supplement the meaning of the first imperative or an earlier statement. An example of a secondary command is, "Abide in me," in John 15:4.

An Example From Matthew 6:1–18

The paragraph begins with the imperative, "Beware of practicing your righteousness... in order to be seen by them...." Within the command are the following verbs/verbals: beware, practicing, and be noticed. The main finite verb is "beware." A broad subject could be worded: being aware of practicing your righteousness before other people.

You try it in Colossians 2:8–15:

Imperative(s):	
Broad Subject:	

Here's how I saw it:

Imperative(s):	"See to it that..."
Broad Subject:	Seeing to it that no one takes you captive.

Finding the Broad Subject in Poetry (Psalms)
Biblical poetry in the Psalms has a unique way of projecting meaning. I've found it helpful to analyze how Psalms begin. Then, as in the previous genre, we locate the main verbs contained within the various introductions.

Description of the Poet's Situation

The opening verses of several Psalms describe the poet's circumstances—what he is facing and feeling. In most of these cases the broad subject is located in the description. For instance, Psalm 137 begins with: "By the waters of Babylon, there we sat down and wept, when we remembered Zion." Meaning in the Psalm hinges on the concept of Israel weeping by the waters.

You try it with Psalm 3:1–8:

Broad Subject:	

Here's how I saw it:

Broad Subject:	David telling God how many foes he has.

What the Poet Says to the Lord (invocation)

Several Psalms begin with the psalmist speaking directly to God. At times, the Psalmist reports his current situation. Sometimes he asks God to do something for him. Psalm 5 opens with, "Give ear to my words, O Lord; consider my groaning." Meaning will be connected to the concept of the Psalmist asking the Lord to hear his words.

Give it a try in Psalm 4:1–8:

Broad Subject:	

Here's how I saw it:

Broad Subject:	David asking the Lord to answer him when he calls.

What the Poet Tells the Worshippers to Do

In Psalm 107:1–2 the poet writes: "Oh give thanks to the LORD, for he is good, for his steadfast love endures forever! Let the redeemed of the LORD say so, whom he has redeemed from trouble…" As the Psalm unfolds, meaning centers on the congregation giving thanks to the Lord.

Give it a try from Psalm 47:

Broad Subject:	

Here's how I saw it:[17]

Broad Subject:	All peoples clapping their hands and shouting to God

What the Poet Says to the Worshippers about God, Themselves, or Reality

Psalm 19 begins, "The heavens declare the glory of God, and the sky above proclaims his handiwork." This opening declaration of the heavens declaring the glory of God will drive the meaning of

---

17 At times Hebrew parallelism allows you to include both main verbs in the broad subject. In this case the second line of the parallelism heightens the meaning of the first line, but does not introduce another subject matter.

Psalm 19. As noted above, Hebrew parallelism allows room to vary the wording of the broad subject. You may opt to choose the heightened wording of the second line.

Give it a try in Psalm 114:

Broad Subject:	

Here's how I saw it:

Broad Subject:	Israel going out from Egypt.

A Note about Chiastic Structure

Before we leave this section on poetry, I want to explain something about chiastic structure. Chiastic structure is a stylistic device employed by biblical writers to communicate ideas. A chiasm is formed in a five-verse preaching portion, for instance, when vv. 1 and 5 and vv. 2 and 4 share common ideas. Verse 3 is the focal point of the chiasm. This placement of an idea at the point of the "V" or the center of the "X" can make one assume that when you've located the point or center, you've located the main point or big idea of the preaching portion.

For instance, Sunukjian writes: "In a chiastic structure, the point of the V is the take-home truth. The innermost thought in the arrangement is the one the author is stressing; it's the dominant concept around which the rest of the material revolves."[18] I'm sug-

---

18 Donald R. Sunukjian, *Invitation to Biblical Preaching: Proclaiming Truth with Clarity and Relevance*, Invitation to Theological Studies Series, 2 (Grand Rapids, Mich.: Kregel Publications, 2007), 185. See also John V.

gesting that the center of the chiasm is the dominant *complement* to the subject of the preaching portion. As you can see from the previous examples, the subject is revealed very early in a preaching portion. Within chiasms this means the outer extremity contains the subject, not the point of the "V" or the center of the "X." The information at the center of the chiasm is being stressed to flesh out the meaning of the subject announced early in the Psalm.

Finding the Broad Subject in Proverbs

The typical proverb—a short, memorable statement—is one of the easiest genres to work with at the broad subject level. Because they are so concise, the proverb itself is the idea.

Identify the Main Verb

In Proverbs 22:2, we read that "The rich and the poor meet together; the LORD is the maker of them all." Meaning develops around the rich and poor meeting together.

Give it a try in Proverbs 11:22:

"Like a gold ring in a pig's snout is a beautiful woman without discretion."

Broad Subject:	

Here's how I saw it:

Broad Subject:	A beautiful woman without discretion being like a ring of gold in a swine's snout.

I decided to focus on the beautiful woman because she is the subject of the teaching. I recommend you try more than one option, so you might create another broad subject that reflects the word-order of the first line of the proverb: a gold ring in a pig's snout being like a beautiful woman without discretion.

Finding the Broad Subject in Visions

Visionary literature is often difficult to interpret because of the symbolic language, not to mention the temptation to interpret according to our theological biases (i.e., our eschatological views influencing the interpretation of Daniel and Revelation). However the task of locating the broad subject is not difficult in visionary preaching portions.

Look for the Main Verb Used in the Interpretation of the Vision

Because of the nature of visionary literature, you can expect to encounter the verb, to see, frequently. As a rule, that verb will not factor into the broad subject. This is similar to our earlier discussion about Paul saying, "I urge you, brothers…." We're really interested in what is being seen, not the act of seeing something.

In many visionary preaching portions, the first main verb occurs in the description of the vision. If an interpretation of the vision follows, select the first main verb in the interpretation section of the preaching portion. Notice the sequence in Zechariah 5:1–3

> "Again I lifted my eyes and saw, and behold, a flying scroll! And he said to me, "What do you see?" I answered, "I see a flying scroll. Its length is twenty cubits, and its width ten cubits." Then he said to me, "This is the curse that goes out over the face of the whole land…."

The first two verbs, "lifted" and "saw," are followed by a description of what Zechariah was seeing. Then the interpretation follows the description: "This is the curse that goes out…" The description of the vision might yield the following broad subject: seeing a flying scroll. I suggest you take the broad subject from the interpretation of the vision: the curse going out over the whole land.

Give it a try in Daniel 7:

Like we saw in Zechariah 5, Daniel 7 opens with a description of the vision (vv. 1–14), followed by the interpretation of the vision (vv. 15–28).

Broad Subject:	

Here's how I saw it:

Broad Subject:	The four kings rising up from the earth.

Some visionary preaching portions contain clear statements about the nature of the vision. Daniel 8:19 reads, "He said, 'Behold, I will make known to you what shall be at the latter end of the indignation, for it refers to the appointed time of the end.'" It is very likely that this explanatory statement will guide our search for the meaning of the vision(s).

Look for a Description of What Is Being Seen

There are times when visionary pericopes do not include an interpretation. Revelation 4:1–11 is an example of an entire chapter devoted to a description of a vision with no interpretation. Verse 2 provides the first look at the vision: "At once I was in the Spirit, and behold, a throne stood in heaven, with one seated on the throne."

Meaning is going to be guided by the thought of a throne standing in heaven with someone seated on it.

Give it a try in Ezekiel 1:1–3:

Broad Subject:	

Here's how I saw it:

Broad Subject:	Ezekiel seeing visions of God while he was among the exiles.

Remember to try some options. For instance, you may have selected: the word of the Lord coming to Ezekiel. You may also have decided that the hand of the Lord coming on Ezekiel is synonymous with him seeing visions of God.

Finding the Broad Subject in Prophecy

Prophetic literature displays meaning similar to New Testament epistles. Within the prophets' writings you will encounter narratives and visions. Adjust your search for the broad subject accordingly. What follows are clues for the sermon-like sections within prophetic literature (i.e., like the oracles).

Look for the Main Verb

Malachi 1:1–3 records the oracle of the word of the Lord to Israel through Malachi: "The oracle of the word of the LORD to Israel by Malachi. 'I have loved you,' says the LORD. But you say, 'How have you loved us?' 'Is not Esau Jacob's brother?' declares the LORD.

'Yet I have loved Jacob but Esau I have hated. I have laid waste his hill country and left his heritage to jackals of the desert.'"

The main verb in v. 2 is "have loved" from which we develop the following broad subject: the Lord loving Israel.

Give it a try from Zephaniah 1:1–6:

Broad Subject:	

Here's how I saw it:

Broad Subject:	The Lord utterly sweeping away everything.

Look for Rhetorical Questions

The use of questions is a prominent feature of the prophets' sermons. Word the broad subject by utilizing the main verb within the question. You may have to choose a verb from multiple questions. For instance Isaiah 40:12–20 contains a series of questions. I identified the broad subject from the wording of the first question in verse 12: the one measuring the waters in the hollow of his hand. You might try the wording of v. 18: [no one] comparing with God. You could try summarizing all the questions into a broad subject such as: God doing the impossible.

Give it a try in Isaiah 53:1–12:

Broad Subject:	

Here's how I saw it:[19]

Broad Subject:	(No one) believing our message.

Look for Commands

Like the writers of the NT epistles, OT prophets often employed imperatives in their oracles or messages to God's people. Commands or imperatives found early in a chapter or paragraph will lead to the discovery of meaning. For example, in Jeremiah 10:1–10, verse 2 contains the command: "Learn not the way of the nations..." The broad subject is simply: Israel not learning the way of the nations.

You may decide to word the broad subject from the second, parallel imperative, "nor be dismayed at the signs of the heavens." The broad subject then might be: not being dismayed at the signs. You may decide to include both concepts in one broad subject phrase.

Give it a try in Joel 2:1–17:

Broad Subject:	

Here's how I saw it:

Broad Subject:	Blowing a trumpet in Zion.

---

19 I've added the negative to show the intent of this rhetorical question. No one had believed Isaiah's message.

You might choose wording from the second line of verse 1. The broad subject would be: sounding an alarm on God's holy mountain.

Finding the Broad Subject in Parables

Note the Repetition of a Word or Action

Repeated words or actions often lead to significant meaning in parables, just as they did in narratives. In Mark 12:1–12, the action of sending occurs in verses 2, 4, 5, and 6. Also, the violent treatment of the ones being sent is repeated. The broad subject could be worded: the vineyard owner sending his servants to the tenants at harvest time.

Give it a try in Matthew 22:1–14:

Broad Subject:	

Here's how I saw it:

Broad Subject:	The kingdom of heaven being compared to a king who gave a wedding feast and sent his servants to invite guests.

Notice the repetition of "invited" in vv. 3, 4, 8, 9 and the repeated action of sending servants to call those who had been invited to the wedding.

Observe the Narrative Occasion of the Parable

Some parables, especially in Luke's Gospel, occur within a narrative context. The narrative controls the meaning of the parable by providing the subject. Luke 15 is an example of this phenomenon.

The first three verses read: "Now the tax collectors and sinners were all drawing near to hear [Jesus]. And the Pharisees and the scribes grumbled, saying, 'This man receives sinners and eats with them.' So he told them this parable…"

Our search for the meaning of the parable begins with analysis of the opening scene. So, you might word the broad subject: Jesus receiving and eating with sinners.[20]

Give it a try from Luke 18:9–14:

Broad Subject:	

Here's how I saw it:

Broad Subject:	Some people trusting in themselves that they were righteous, and treating others with contempt.

The broad subject phrase comes directly from v. 9, the narrative occasion for the parable.

Identify the summary statement by Jesus (the Rule of End Stress[21])

There are times when the way a parable ends encapsulates its meaning. Take, for example, Matthew 21:28–32 which ends with,

---

20 I'll refer to this parable again in a later section, but I'd like to point out that this initial meaning influences the application of the parable by focusing on the older brother, not the younger brother. Most sermons on Luke 15 end with a call to prodigals to come home. That application is the result of interpretation that has neglected the opening narrative setup.

21 Ryken, *How to Read the Bible as Literature*, 142.

"'Which of the two did the will of his father?' They said, 'The first.' Jesus said to them, 'Truly, I say to you, the tax collectors and the prostitutes go into the kingdom of God before you...'"

As you saw from previous examples, normally it's wise to look for the broad subject early in the preaching portion. That is not the only way to operate in some parables. In this parable I might word the broad subject: doing the will of his father. You might decide to focus on the second part of v. 31 where Jesus says, "Truly I say to you that the tax collectors and prostitutes will get into the kingdom of God before you." The broad subject then would read: tax collectors and prostitutes getting into the kingdom of God before the religious leaders.

Give it a try in Matthew 21:33–46:

Broad Subject:	

Here's how I saw it:

Broad Subject:	The kingdom of God being taken away from the chief priests and the Pharisees.

The wording of the broad subject comes from Jesus' summary statement in verse 43. Be prepared to attempt to word another broad subject from the beginning of the parable. You may discover that the summary statement at the end of the parable functions as a complement to a subject that began at the beginning of the parable. In this case the broad subject is worded according to the action of the tenants mistreating the master's servants. Jesus' summary statement explains what happens as a result of the tenants mistreating the master's servants. At this stage of study it's often helpful to try more than one option. You can check yourself as you proceed with sermon development.

The Value of Finding the Broad Subject

As I said at the beginning of this section, identifying the broad subject is the first step in beginning to decipher meaning. All other exegetical and theological endeavors build on this foundation. The search for the broad subject begins to reveal the relationship between the multiple meanings that reside in a preaching portion. This allows pastors to make decisions on how they will communicate the Text. It provides an opportunity to choose whether they'll emphasize a small or larger idea. This helps us be intentional about the choices all of us make whenever we preach the Bible.

2. Write the Narrow Subject

Writing out the broad subject is an attempt to capture the general direction of meaning within a preaching portion. Identifying the narrowed subject attempts to narrow meaning so that it more precisely reflects what the preaching portion is saying. To narrow the broad subject, the phrase morphs into one of seven questions. Robinson writes: "Applying these six questions to your proposed subject will help you be more exact."[22] I've found that the "what" question can be phrased in two ways: "what it means…" and "what is the result of…." Here's what the seven questions look like from my analysis of Romans 6:1–11. The broad subject might be worded, "Christians (not) continuing in sin," which yields the following narrowed subjects:

- How Christians should not continue in sin…?
- What (it means that) Christians should not continue in sin…?
- What (is the result) of Christians not continuing in sin…?
- Why Christians should not continue in sin…?

---

22 Robinson, *Biblical Preaching: The Development and Delivery of Expository Messages*, 67. The six interrogatives are: how, what, why, when, where, who.

- When Christians should not continue in sin...?
- Where Christians should not continue in sin...?
- Who should not continue in sin...?

Let's be clear on what these questions are asking. The "how" question focuses on a method whereby Christians can stop sinning continually. The "what" questions focus on either what it means to not continue in sin or the result of not continuing in sin. The "why" question focuses on a rationale or reason for Christians not continuing in sin. The "when" question focuses on some time frame for Christians not continuing in sin. The "where" question focuses on geography or location. The "who" question focuses on the individuals involved.

It is not always easy to formulate these seven questions. I can't even offer any helpful rules; practice does seem to make perfect (well, almost perfect).

Give it a try in Hebrews 1:1–14 using
the broad subject—God speaking to us:

How...	
What is the result...	
What does it mean...	
Why...	
When...	
Where...	
Who...	

Here's how I saw it:

How...	...God is speaking to us?
What is the result...	...of God speaking to us?
What does it mean...	...that God is speaking to us?
Why...	...God is speaking to us?
When...	...God is speaking to us?
Where...	...God is speaking to us?
Who...	...is God speaking to? (This is an awkward question and an example of times when the answer is already contained in the other questions.)

3. Write the Complement(s)

Robinson writes: "A subject cannot stand alone. By itself it is incomplete, and therefore it needs a complement. The complement 'completes' the subject by answering the question, 'What am I saying about what I am talking about?'"[23] The complements are the preaching portion's answer to the narrowed subject questions. Begin at the beginning of the preaching portion and proceed line by line. Record any answer provided for each question using the wording of your English Bible. These answers complete the narrowed subjects you've created.

I suggested the following broad subject for Romans 6:1–11: Christians not continuing in sin. I also wrote out seven narrowed

---

23 *Biblical Preaching: The Development and Delivery of Expository Messages*, 41.

subject questions. Now it's time to see how the paragraph answers each question. Here's what I discovered:

- How Christians should not continue in sin? There is no method given.
- What (it means that) Christians should not continue in sin? The Text doesn't explain.
- Why Christians should not continue in sin? Christians are "dead to sin" (v. 2), "baptized into Jesus Christ..." (v. 3), "buried with Him..." (v. 4), "planted together..." (v. 5), "our old man is crucified..." (v. 6), and "death hath no more dominion over him..." (v. 9).
- When Christians should not continue in sin? Nothing is said about a particular time, but it's assumed that Christians should never continue in sin.
- Where Christians should not continue in sin? Nothing is said about a particular place, but the assumed answer would be "everywhere."
- Who should not continue in sin? The implied answer is "all Christians."

The result of this analysis is we now have an idea of what this paragraph communicates. The emphasis lies with the "why" question. The presence of multiple answers gives us the option of either summarizing our findings ("...because our identification with Christ's burial makes us dead to sin") or selecting one of the answers above for our complement ("...because Christians are dead to sin").

There is no interpreting going on at this phase. I don't know what the biblical data means yet. What I do know is how the various sized ideas connect. Primary meaning is displayed through the relationship between the narrowed subject (why Christians should not continue in sin) and the complement (because of our identification with Christ's death).

Some preaching portions will answer more than one question. The exercise of creating and answering the seven questions helps us see other ideas contained in the preaching portion. This is especially important in determining which idea is more dominant. Other ideas may form major and minor points or movements within the sermon.

Give it a try in Hebrews 1:1–14. Earlier I suggested the broad subject, "God speaking to us," and crafted the narrowed subject questions. Begin at verse 1 and proceed line-by-line through the section, listing all answers provided.

Here's how I saw it:

How God is speaking to us?	Verse 2 says, "by His Son."
What (is the result of) God speaking to us?	No answer.
What (does it mean that) God is speaking to us?	No answer.
Why is God speaking to us?	No reason is provided.
When is God speaking to us?	Verse 2 says, "in these last days."
Where is God speaking to us?	No location is provided.
Who (or to whom) is God speaking to us?	Verse 2 says, "to us."

Once the answers are recorded, look for the one that is most prominent. Look for the question that is answered most in the preaching portion. Rule out the questions that are not answered (the "where," "why," and "what" questions) and the redundant ones ("to whom" is contained in the broad subject so it can be eliminated). With some practice you'll quickly identify the one or two more prominent subjects and complements.

In this case verse 2 provides an answer to the "how" and "when" questions. The "how" question is the best choice because the answer, "by his Son," dominates the preaching portion. Everything from the middle of v. 2 on (beginning with the relative pronoun, "whom…") describes the Son through whom God is speaking. Nothing further in the preaching portion fleshes out the "when" question.

4. Write the Textual Big Idea

The textual big idea is formed by combining the narrowed subject question with the complement's answer. Look at our example from Romans 6:1–11:

$$\text{narrowed subject} + \text{complement} = \text{textual big idea}$$

Broad Subject:	Christians (not) continuing in sin
Narrowed Subject:	Why Christians shouldn't continue in sin
Complement:	because they are dead to sin
Textual Big Idea (texbi):	Christians shouldn't continue in sin because they are dead to sin.

Our example from Hebrews 1:1–14
might develop as follows:

Broad Subject:	God speaking to us
Narrowed Subject:	How is God speaking to us?
Complement:	by His Son
Textual Big Idea (texbi):	God is speaking to us by His Son.

Try it with 1 Peter 3:7:

> "Likewise, husbands, live with your wives in an understanding way, showing honor to the woman as the weaker vessel, since they are heirs with you of the grace of life, so that your prayers may not be hindered."

Broad Subject:	
Narrowed Subject:	
Complement:	
Textual Big Idea (texbi):	

Here's how I saw it:

Broad Subject:	Broad Subject: husbands living with your wives in an understanding way
Narrowed Subject:	Narrowed Subject: why husbands should live with their wives in an understanding way
Complement:	Complement: so that their prayers will not be hindered
Textual Big Idea (texbi):	Texbi: Husbands are to live with their wives in an understanding way so their prayers will not be hindered.

The benefit of stating the texbi is discovering the logical connection between the ideas. We begin to see how the parts fit the whole. Remember to list more than one option and allow the rest of your sermon preparation to help you confirm or adjust your texbi.

Notice that, in most of the examples above, the subject occurs early in the preaching portion. Then, the first complement appears. The texbi sounds identical to the early part of the preaching portion. The rest of the subject is fleshed out in the rest of the passage. Now, you're in a position to decide whether to preach big or little ideas.

5

IDENTIFYING THE CONTEXTUAL BIG IDEA (CONBI)

In the previous chapter I provided a method for preachers to identify the textual big idea of a selected preaching portion. This means that an informed choice can now be made concerning how to craft the sermon. We can choose to highlight the dominant idea in the preaching portion or we can choose to focus on a subordinate idea. We know how the various sized ideas interrelate to form meaning. This goes a long way toward helping us interpret the Text. It's a good start. The Text is important, but so is the context.

Vanhoozer notes, "The prime rule for hermeneutics, as in real estate, is 'location, location, location.' In the case of determining meaning, 'location' means context."[1] You know how this works in

---

1   Kevin J. Vanhoozer, *Is There a Meaning in This Text?: The Bible, the Reader, and the Morality of Literary Knowledge* (Grand Rapids, Mich.: Zondervan, 1998), 112. Silva puts it even more strongly: "the context does not merely help us understand meaning; it virtually *makes* meaning." Cf. *Is There a Meaning in This Text?*, 250.

every day communication. The word *hog* means one thing in the context of farming, another thing in the context of siblings arguing at the dining room table, and another thing in the context of motorcycles. It could be argued that, at times, context makes meaning.

Preaching portions are often under- or over-interpreted due to a neglect of their immediate context. Under-interpretation occurs when pastors state meaning that is biblical, but not biblical enough. The meaning of the preaching portion is accurate, but partial. More meaning resides in the immediate context. Take the well-known parable of the Compassionate Samaritan in Luke 10:25–37. By itself, God certainly means for His children to follow the example of the Samaritan ("And Jesus said to [the lawyer], 'You go, and do likewise.'"). In the immediate context, the lawyer is an example of "the wise and understanding" from whom God hides the fact that His Kingdom has arrived in the person of Jesus (cf. Luke 10:21).

Preaching portions are over-interpreted when pastors state meaning that is beyond-biblical. Had the immediate context been consulted, the preacher would have encountered controls on meaning.[2] An example might be an emphasis on the priesthood of the believer that does away with any need for pastoral authority (cf. 1 Peter 2:9 "…a royal priesthood" and 1 Peter 5:2 "shepherd the flock of God…").

So early on in our study we want to consult the immediate context of our preaching portion. If we're preaching in Exodus 4, for instance, we want to ask how the book of Exodus fleshes out the meaning of our narrative. Here's what we're looking for.

- The definition of key terms and concepts or an on-going plot that is a vital part of the textual big idea. If you're preaching through a book of the Bible from start to finish,

---

2   Refer to chapter 2 for other examples of how context affects meaning. Davis suggests that, "the 'large view' becomes a kind of control that keeps me from abusing or twisting individual passages." Cf. Dale Ralph Davis, *The Word Became Fresh: How to Preach from Old Testament Narrative Texts* (Fearn, Ross-shire, Scotland: Christian Focus, 2006), 84.

you will encounter these definitions as they occur in the book. However, if you find yourself in the middle of a book, you may be unaware of earlier, significant meanings of key terms and concepts or place-in-plot.

- The logical, thematic connections between our preaching portion and the larger biblical narrative. We're asking how our preaching portion fits within the logical development of the biblical book in which it is found. We're investigating how our preaching portion contributes to the book (e.g., how the bizarre story of Exodus 4:24–26 fits into the Exodus narrative). This type of analysis has a significant bearing on meaning because often a book's overall purpose supplies individual preaching portions with theology for the Church.

What follows are some observations I have found helpful in allowing the immediate context to influence the meaning of a preaching portion. I'll begin with general observations about the Old Testament, Gospels (and Acts), and New Testament Epistles, and then move to more specific observations about segments within those broad sections of Scripture.[3]

The Unique Characteristics of Three Major Sections of the Bible

Two Unique Characteristics of Old Testament Literature

1. God Is the Main Character
It is easy to forget that God is the main character because of

---

3   I am using these three, broad categories of OT, Gospels, and NT Epistles knowing that there are other, more detailed classifications. My purpose is to suggest characteristics that help determine meaning for large blocks of biblical text.

the presence of so many major-looking, but minor-leading characters that monopolize action. Not to mention a book such as Esther where God is seemingly absent. No matter where you are in an OT narrative, consider looking out for what Wilson calls the "God sense" of a preaching portion.[4] Wilson adamantly concludes that "exegesis that leaves God out misinterprets the scriptural message."[5] Remember what I said earlier about under-interpreting a preaching portion? Exegesis built on the perspective of God being the major character opens interpretation to other, fruitful options.

2. Narrative Rules the Larger Context

Like the Bible as a whole, the Old Testament tells a story. It begins at creation, moves quickly into de-creation, proceeds with seeds of re-creation, and ends with prophetic peeps at the new creation (cf. Isaiah 65:17; 66:22; Malachi 3–4). This narrative context is the framework within which OT preaching portions are interpreted and applied. A prime example of this is how the Exodus narrative affects the interpretation of the Ten Commandments.

First, all the laws are preceded by God's redemption of His people. The laws explain how redeemed people live. Obedience is the result of redemption, not the cause. Second, the preceding narrative explains what obedience to God's laws accomplishes. Obedience to the law of God creates a holy people that represent God in the world (cf. Exodus 19:5–6). Even when individual laws may no longer apply to us due to our place in redemptive history (such as some of the dietary restrictions), the Law as a whole applies. God chose to enhance His reputation in the Church and in the world through the redeemed lifestyle.

---

4   Paul Scott Wilson, *God Sense: Reading the Bible for Preaching* (Nashville: Abingdon Press, 2001). Wilson laments, "our ways of reading [the Bible] have not always led us to God." Cf. *God Sense: Reading the Bible for Preaching* (Nashville: Abingdon Press, 2001), 8.
5   Ibid., 66.

Two Unique Characteristics of the Gospels

1. The Interplay between Various Genres

You don't have to read too many pages in the Gospels to discover that they contain several kinds of genre. Matthew's gospel opens with a genealogy. Soon you're reading narrative, mixed with hymns or poetry. Then Matthew mentions more stories, teaching sections, parables, and prophecy.[6] We learned earlier that different genres convey meaning differently.

Be on the lookout for preaching portions that contain more than one genre. Understanding how genres work together to communicate meaning is a key interpretive step when preaching in the Gospels. You'll encounter this in at least two scenarios: (1) many of Jesus' parables in the gospel of Luke are embedded in the context of a narrative; the narrative provides the subject of the big idea, not the parable; (2) some narrative sections function as an illustration to a previous teaching section. In those cases the narrative contains no theme of its own, but was designed to complement a theme announced in the broader context. Some of Jesus' healing stories fit into this category.

2. The Main Character Is Jesus

In the same way that God is the main character in the OT, Jesus is the main character in the Gospels. As a rule, then, that makes all the other characters in the Gospels, minor characters. Christ will be the focus of our sermons even if another strong character seems

---

6   For a helpful look at the genres and sub-genres within the Gospels, see Leland Ryken, *How to Read the Bible as Literature,* 137. Vanhoozer states, "David Aune . . . lists twenty different genres that he finds in the Gospels alone, including sayings of Jesus, proverbs, parables, miracle stories, genealogies, and prayers. These are best described, however, as 'sub-genres,' for they are embedded within an overarching narrative and are subordinate to the text as a whole; they have a relative independence only." Cf. Vanhoozer, *Is There a Meaning in This Text?: The Bible, the Reader, and the Morality of Literary Knowledge,* 349.

to dominate the preaching portion.[7] This means we will need to re-think how we preach exemplar sermons (in the case of following a good example of a character, "go and do likewise;" or in the case of avoiding the bad example of a character, "go and do otherwise").

Two Unique Characteristics of New Testament Epistles[8]

1. Structured Around an Argument (Line of Reasoning)
Epistles are structured around a logical flow or line of reasoning. Some paragraphs contain meaning independent of the larger context. Often, however, paragraphs connect logically and thematically to form larger sections within an epistle. These larger sections form the immediate context for any preaching portions within them. Preaching with greater accuracy involves identifying the author's line of reasoning and connecting our preaching portion to that line of reasoning.

2. Common Authorship Creates a Context beyond One Letter
Since Paul, for instance, wrote thirteen books, you'll discover that he uses similar vocabulary and also similar lines of reasoning. If you're studying Galatians you will find help defining terms such as "righteousness" in Romans (or vice versa). In more than one letter,

---

7   Although anti-exemplar preaching, Greidanus suggests helpful guidelines for preaching minor characters. Cf. Greidanus, *The Modern Preacher and the Ancient Text*, 290, 305–06. You might also benefit from reading Busenitz's brief treatment of biographical preaching where he stresses the need to focus on the sovereign workings of God in the life of a minor character. Cf. John MacArthur, *Rediscovering Expository Preaching* (Dallas: Word, 1992), 270–71.
8   "Scott Hafemann urges the preacher to consider at least five characteristics in the epistles that will affect our exposition of them. These are the theological character, the occasional nature, the discursive structure, the central thrust, and the imperative exhortations." Cf. Graeme Goldsworthy, *Preaching the Whole Bible as Christian Scripture: The Application of Biblical Theology to Expository Preaching* (Grand Rapids, Mich.: W.B. Eerdmans, 2000), 243.

Paul writes about the unity of the Church. At times, the meaning of a preaching portion in one Pauline epistle may be fleshed out by the broader context provided from another.

The Immediate Context of the Old Testament

The Covenants Provide Structure and Meaning

Even though different theological camps view the covenants differently, no one can dismiss the importance of God's covenants to biblical interpretation. The covenants contain vital information about God's relationship with His people. But our interest centers on how they affect the meaning of many OT preaching portions. Most OT narratives function within the context of one covenant or another. Often, this means we discover a fuller meaning of a preaching portion when a narrative is interpreted in light of the covenant God made with His people.

Repeated, Theologically Loaded Vocabulary

Repeated key words and concepts within a book of the Bible often flesh out meaning for your selected preaching portion. At times a mini-narrative, such as the bizarre story of Judah and Tamar recorded in Genesis 38, is impossible to understand until you consult the larger context. In the first chapter of his book, Alter spends a significant amount of space tracing how this mini-narrative is intended to function within the larger narrative.[9] He shows how the Judah/Tamar narrative shares vocabulary with the immediate context (cf. the Hebrew verbs translated "examine" and "recognize" in Genesis 37:33; 38:25–26).

You might also notice the repeated action that moves Judah from being a deceiver to being deceived. These connections help reveal how the seemingly out of place story functions as an exam-

---

9   Robert Alter, *The Art of Biblical Narrative* (New York: Basic Books, 1981), 3–22.

ple of God turning evil into good (cf. the purpose statement for the entire Joseph narrative in Genesis 50:20).

Look for the Story within the Story

When we choose to preach a narrative in the Old Testament, it may appear to have a sufficient level of independence. It has a background, rising action, climax, and conclusion. The example above, however, shows that the larger narrative may supply theological meaning. The long narrative in Genesis portraying the life of Joseph is an example of several mini-narratives working together to communicate theology for the Church. The Joseph story is also an excellent example of how meaning morphs with expanding contexts. Enjoy the following analysis by Carson:

> ...little narratives should not only be interpreted within the framework of the book in which they are embedded, but within the corpus, and ultimately within the canon. Take, for instance, Genesis 39, the account of Joseph's early years in Egypt. One can read that narrative and draw from it excellent lessons on how to resist temptation.... But a careful reading of the opening and closing verses of the chapter also shows that one of the important points of the narrative is that God is with Joseph and blesses him even in the midst of the most appalling circumstances: neither the presence of God nor the blessing of God are restricted to happy lifestyles. Then read the chapter in the context of the preceding narrative: now Judah becomes a foil for Joseph. The one is tempted in circumstances of comfort and plenty, and succumbs to incest; the other is tempted in circumstances of slavery and injustice, and retains his integrity. Now read the same chapter in the context of the book of Genesis. Joseph's integrity is bound

up with the way God providentially provides famine relief not only for countless thousands, but for the covenant people of God in particular. Now read it within the context of the Pentateuch. The narrative is part of the explanation for how the people of God find themselves in Egypt, which leads to the Exodus. Joseph's bones are brought out when the people leave. Enlarge the horizon now to embrace the whole canon: suddenly Joseph's fidelity in small matters is part of the providential wisdom that preserves the people of God, leads to the exodus that serves as a type of a still greater release, and ultimately leads to Judah's distant son David, and his still more distant son, Jesus.

So if you are applying Genesis 39, although it may have some use as a moral account that tells us how to deal with temptation, the perspective gained by admitting the widening contexts discloses scores of further connections and meanings that thoughtful readers (and preachers) should not ignore.[10]

Carson's analysis is extremely helpful; we've grown accustomed to that, haven't we? I want us to gain a bit more specificity, though. It's true. We should not ignore the scores of further connections and meanings added by widening our contexts. But what does this mean for any given sermon?

Well, first, such discussions about widening contexts and fleshed-out meaning always result in students or workshop participants asking: "But, do we have to do this analysis every time we preach an OT narrative? Do we have to create that breadcrumb trail of meaning in every sermon?" My answers are, yes and no.

---

10 D. A. Carson, "The Tabula Rasa Fallacy: Why We Must Become Self-Conscious about Our Interpretation," *Modern Reformation* 8, no. 4 (1999): 31–32.

I've already suggested that we should interpret preaching portions in light of their immediate and canonical contexts. Take a moment and reread Carson's analysis of the Genesis narrative. Look at how different the meaning of the isolated story is from its fleshed-out meaning in context. From a human perspective, which meaning are you satisfied with preaching? From a Divine perspective, which meaning is God focused on? The purely moralistic interpretation and application—when you're tempted, be like Joseph—is valid only within the context of the larger meaning and application. So, yes, interpret and apply in context.

But, no, I do not believe it's best to lay out the entire breadcrumb trail in every sermon. At least not as detailed as Carson's example above. In that example I'm suggesting a sermon needs to include the contrast between Joseph and Judah, and that Joseph's integrity leads to Judah's distant Son. We will discuss this in more detail in the next chapter. For now, I'm asking you to consider how the moral example of Joseph means something in light of the larger context of God saving His people. Ultimately, our only hope for following Joseph's example and avoiding Judah's example is found in faith in Judah's distant Son.[11]

Allow the Narrative to Rule the Immediate Context

Consider again Exodus 20, the list the Ten Commandments. Rather than being interpreted as individual commands, read them as part the larger story of the redemption of Israel from Egypt. In particular the commandments are found within the context of the account of God giving the Law to Moses that begins in chapter 19 and continues to chapter 24. The Ten Commandments find their meaning within this context. Isolate any one commandment and

---

11 You can see that I am not pitting exemplar preaching against Christ-centered or redemptive-historical preaching. I believe both have their place in the narrative. I also believe the contextual meaning and application (trust Judah's Son) provide the foundation for the textual meaning and application (follow Joseph's example).

the sermon will explain what the commandment means and possibly how to perform it.

What is missing is the reason why God gave the commandment. The immediate context contains the reason. Cf. Exodus 19:5–6: "and you shall be to me a kingdom of priests and a holy nation...." This describes God's people when they obey His commandments. The same is true of other law sections in the OT, the poetry of Moses' song (Exodus 15), or Nebuchadnezzar's dreams recorded in Daniel. They contain meaning by themselves; they mean more within the context of the larger narrative. The larger narrative determines how the laws, song, or dreams are designed to function.

An Example of Contextual Interpretation from Genesis 20:1–18 (the story of Abraham lying about Sarah and Sarah being taken by King Abimelech)

I've summarized the story into the following texbi:

> The result of Abraham saying that Sarah was his
> sister, was Abimelech takes Sarah, is punished
> by God, restores Sarah, and is healed by God in
> response to Abraham's prayer.

The textual big idea simply shows the logical relationship between the scenes of the narrative. I do not yet know what this story means. So, let's turn our attention to the immediate context.

First, God is the main character, even though Abraham is featured. Abraham is acting in light of something God has done. Abraham enters Gerar having heard and believed God's earlier promises.

Second, this isolated narrative relates logically and thematically to the larger narrative in Genesis. In Genesis, God creates the world and the human race and provides for redemption through a chosen people. They are called to believe His promises and obey His laws.

Moses writes to God's people and urges them to continue to believe that God will keep His promise. Abraham is having a tough time believing this.

Apparently, Abraham doesn't think the promise can come true without lying. God has promised Abraham that he would bear a son through Sarah. Abraham's actions in Genesis 20 reveal a lack of faith in God's ability to keep His promise. God's promise to Abraham can't be fulfilled if Abimelech kills Abraham to get Sarah.

Finally, when we turn our attention to a more detailed analysis of the immediate context, we discover repeated concepts and terms. For instance, chapter 19 ends with Lot's seed being preserved through deception and manipulation. From the end of chapter 19 through chapter 21 there is the repetition of bearing children (cf. 19:37–38; 20:17–18; 21:2). In Genesis 12:7 God's promise to Abraham involves a "seed."

Abraham and Sarah have struggled throughout with this promise (i.e. Hagar in chapter 16). This analysis shows that the story in Genesis 20 is not only a warning against lying. When Abraham lies, he reveals his lack of faith in God's promise. This narrative functions as a call for God's people to believe His promises and be confident that He will intervene to keep His promises. That faith inevitably leads to truth-telling.[12]

How does this contextual interpretation affect the wording of our texbi? We began with:

> The result of Abraham saying that Sarah was his
> sister was Abimelech takes Sarah, is punished
> by God, restores Sarah, and is healed by God in
> response to Abraham's prayer.

---

12 Notice, again, that the exemplar—avoiding Abraham's example ("go and do otherwise")—has its place. Again, faith in God's promised salvation is the foundation for the moral lesson. It's not either/or, but both/and.

A contextual big idea (conbi) might be:

> The result of Abraham not trusting in God's
> promise was that God's plan to bless Abraham
> and the nations through Abraham is temporarily
> jeopardized, but God intervenes and allows
> Abraham to function as a prophet who heals
> Abimelech and his household.[13]

Davis implements this reading strategy in her analysis of Genesis 22. She writes, "If Abraham goes his own way, if he tries to secure his own life apart from God's plan, then all God's hope of overcoming our evil is lost. If Abraham holds back anything at all from God, even the child Isaac, if Abraham is not wholehearted toward God, then the light of divine blessing cannot pass through him to bathe and reinvigorate our world.... That is what this terrible test is about."[14]

The Immediate Context of the Gospels

Like many Old Testament narratives, Gospel narratives mean something in light of the larger context. Textual interpretation means one thing; contextual interpretation means more. In the Gospels, individual scenes, acts, and stories are woven together to make theological statements.[15] In addition, the Gospels also contain lessons or teaching sections that work in conjunction with surrounding narratives.

Alter argues that OT exegetes must assume "that the Text is an intricately interconnected unity" rather than assuming that "it is

---

13　Often the evolution of an idea from textbi to conbi lengthens it as pertinent contextual information is added. Additional lengthening may also occur in moving from conbi to canbi.

14　Ellen F. Davis and Richard B. Hays, *The Art of Reading Scripture* (Grand Rapids, Mich.: Eerdmans, 2003).

15　Greidanus, *The Modern Preacher and the Ancient Text*, 285.

a patchwork of frequently disparate documents."[16] I'm suggesting the same is true for the Gospels. This connection of text and context requires an analysis of the context in order to preach the Text with greater accuracy. So, what are we looking for in the immediate context of the Gospels?

Repetition of Key Terms or Concepts

Sections of a Gospel are often held together by a common theme. Alter calls this phenomenon in the OT, "verbal signals of continuity."[17] The meaning of gospel preaching portions is often enhanced through a study of the repetition of key terms or concepts within the immediate context. Locating repetitive elements does two things: (1) provide helpful insight for defining terms in your preaching portion; (2) steer the meaning of the entire preaching portion in a certain direction, a direction that wasn't totally clear from the preaching portion itself.

Take for instance the three-part parable of Luke 15. If we expand our view of the immediate context to chapters 14 (see vv. 7, 12, 14, 33) and 16 (see vv. 1, 13, 14) we'll see Jesus condemning the Pharisees for their love of position and money. This sheds more light on the stories Jesus uses to confront the Pharisees on their lack of compassion for the lost in chapter 15. Finding the lost sheep would have appealed to the Pharisees' value of economics. It's the same with the story of the lost coin, and even with the lost son who forsakes his position and squanders his wealth. An analysis of the immediate context helps us see that one main problem with the Pharisees was that they didn't value sinners like God does.

Teaching Sections within the Immediate Context

Martin Luther once wrote, "where narrative and message stand together, we take the message to be more important. And this is in

---

16 Alter, *The Art of Biblical Narrative*, 11.
17 Ibid. In Matthew 13:54–19:2 this connectedness is revealed through the recurrence of the terms "offend" and "offenses."

fact a rule: To interpret the Gospels correctly, we must pay attention to what is spoken, particularly by Christ."[18] If your preaching portion is a narrative or parable it may be important to check the immediate context to see if there is some verbal or thematic connection to a nearby teaching section.[19]

Mark 8:22–26 contains the story of Jesus healing the blind man of Bethsaida. Because the narrative has rising action and a climax, one might think that the story can be preached alone. In the immediate context of vv. 14–21, Jesus questions his disciples about the significance of the miracle of the loaves. Jesus' disciples were struggling to see or understand (notice the repetition in vv. 17, 18, 21).[20]

The gradual, clearing vision of the blind man anticipates Jesus' disciples gradually seeing more clearly who He was and what He had come to do (8:27–30). Notice the emphasis on seeing in vv. 22–26. The instruction gives meaning to the story. The miracle story in vv. 22–26 serves as an illustration of the gradual development of the disciples' understanding. Even when it appeared Peter saw Jesus clearly, Peter's confession ("You are the Christ") did not keep him from rebuking Jesus' prophecy about the cross (vv. 31–33). Peter still wasn't seeing as clearly as he needed to.

Narratives That Serve as Illustrations

When a narrative seems dependent on a didactic section, look to see if the narrative is functioning as an illustration. There are times when a narrative is not designed to be preached alone; it is dependent on the larger context for its meaning. Fee and Stuart note that, "stories...are placed in a context of teaching, where the story itself serves as an il-

---

18 Martin Luther, *The Complete Sermons of Martin Luther,* 7 vols., vol. 6 (Grand Rapids, Mich.: Baker, 2000), 60.

19 McCartney and Clayton's second priority of interpretation is "a didactic or systematic discussion of a subject is more significant for that subject than a historical or descriptive narrative." Cf. McCartney and Clayton, *Let the Reader Understand,* 207.

20 This example from Mark's Gospel also reinforces the need to check the immediate context for the repetition of key terms and concepts.

lustration of what is being taught."[21] To preach that story would result in only preaching an illustration, not the meaning being illustrated.

Consider the narrative sections in Luke 18:15–27. The first story shows Jesus' reaction to infants being brought to Him (vv. 15–17). The second story records Jesus' encounter with a law-abiding ruler (vv. 18–27). Both narratives follow Christ's teaching in Luke 18:9–14, a parable with explicit purpose (v. 9 says, "He also told this parable to some who trusted in themselves that they were righteous, and treated others with contempt" and v. 14 states, "For everyone who exalts himself will be humbled, but the one who humbles himself will be exalted"). The two following stories provide a positive and negative illustration of the earlier teaching about who receives justification from God.

If you are preaching through the Gospel of Luke and land on the story of Jesus permitting the children to come to Him, keep in mind that the story is intended to be an illustration of the humble being exalted. To ignore this connection could result in presenting meaning that Luke never intended. It's easy to do because the story has a beginning, middle, and end and possesses its own plot and characters—all the makings of a complete story. But the story does not have its own theological meaning apart from the larger context.

Parables That Begin or End a Section

Parables sometimes serve as literary anchors of meaning. Just like instructional portions, the parable, with its explanation by Jesus, can control meaning in the immediate context. An example of this is Luke 18:9–14 that we looked at above. Jesus tells the parable to those who trust in themselves that they are righteous and scorn others. The parable illustrates how trusting in oneself leads to humiliation, but trusting in God's mercy results in exaltation. The following narratives all have "trust in self" or "trust in the mercy of God" at the heart of their story.

---

21 Fee and Stuart, *How to Read the Bible for All Its Worth*, 118.

The story of helpless little children being brought to Christ demonstrates trust in God's mercy, while the young ruler trusts in his riches (Luke 18:15–30). Both the blind man near Jericho who asks Jesus for mercy (18:35–43) and Zaccheus, who proves that he is no longer trusting in his riches (Luke19:1–10), are examples of those who trust in the mercy of God. The parable of the Pharisee and the tax collector encourages us to see the following narratives as developing Jesus' teaching about what happens to those who exalt themselves and to those who humble themselves. Preaching with greater accuracy involves seeing this interconnection between narratives and parables.

An Example of Contextual Interpretation from Matthew 4:1–11
(Jesus being led up by the Spirit into the wilderness to be tempted by the devil)

The textual big idea (texbi), which displays the relationship between the parts of the narrative, might be worded:

> The result of Jesus being led by the Spirit into the wilderness to be tempted by the devil was that Jesus cited Scripture, Satan was dismissed, and Jesus was ministered to by the angels.

At this point we have not interpreted the story; we have no real meaning yet. Goldingay reminds us that "Historical events are not self-interpreting.... Something must be given in addition to the events...."[22] In addition to this summary of events, pastors must explain why this event happened to Jesus and what it means

---

22 John Goldingay, "That You May Know That Yahweh Is God: A Study in the Relationship between Theology and Historical Truth in the Old Testament," *Tyndale Bulletin* 23 (1972): 62. Later, on page 68 he writes, "Events, even when regarded as the works of God, are mute or ambiguous. If lessons are to be learned from them, then they must be explained."

for the Church. The preaching portion doesn't tell us, but the context does.

In this case it is important to see the temptation of Christ within the framework of Matthew's theme and purpose for writing. It is helpful to track Matthew's use of "Son of God," a phrase repeated in the temptation narrative. In 1:20–25 we find repeated references to Jesus being a Son (of David and of God). The same is true in 2:15 ("Out of Egypt I called My Son") and in 3:17 ("This is My beloved Son..."). This same theme will appear in 8:29 where the demons address Jesus as "Son of God." In 16:16 Peter calls Jesus "Son of God." In 26:63 Jesus affirms to the high priest that He is the Son of God. In 27:40 Jesus is mocked, "If you are the Son of God," which is identical to Satan's temptation. In 27:43 there is more mocking and quoting Jesus as saying "I am the Son of God." In 27:54 the centurion claims, "Truly this was the Son of God."

Matthew is clearly emphasizing Jesus' true identity and the temptation scene is a part of this. The devil helps the reader learn about Jesus' true identity during the temptation. Meaning now could be expanded into: The result of Jesus successfully defeating the devil's temptation was that He proved His Sonship and His ability to bring about God's kingdom.[23]

The Immediate Context within NT Epistles

Conducting contextual interpretation for New Testament epistles involves the same basic format above. We look to clues from the

---

23 Notice that there is no emphasis on *how* Jesus defeated the devil. The most popular meaning of this story is that Jesus' encounter with the devil teaches us how Christians can defeat temptation. We moralize Jesus' method of quoting appropriate Scripture: "Christians can defeat the devil in times of temptation by quoting appropriate Scripture." While that may be true, we know from Matthew's emphasis that he was not focusing on that. There is a great difference between saying, "You can defeat the devil's temptations by utilizing appropriate Scripture" and "Since Jesus, the Son of God, defeated the devil, we can defeat temptation as we rely on Him."

immediate context to help us explore what the epistolary writers meant by what they said to their audience.

Determining Your Place in the Flow of the Argument

If you choose a preaching portion somewhere in the middle of an epistle, remember that you're breaking into the middle of a tightly woven argument. In those cases, go backwards to find out whether the selected preaching portion contains a new topic or is part of an earlier discussion. I often practice working my way backward in the letter, backtracking the author's flow of thought.

As you pay attention to grammatical connectors, such as conjunctions, you will see whether your preaching portion is influenced by a previous idea. For example, Ephesians contains a few paragraphs in chapters 5 and 6 which, although can be preached individually, all find meaning as they are connected to the flow of argument found in an earlier context (cf. Eph. 5:15–21 and its affect on the instruction given to wives, husbands, children and fathers, and slaves and masters; the specific instructions to various categories of people are designed to illustrate how wise Christians live under the control of the Spirit).

Repeated Key Terms, Concepts, and Metaphors

Tracing the use of terms, concepts, and metaphors establishes a context in which we find meaning for selected preaching portions. For instance, in chapters 4 and 5 of Ephesians, there is a concentration of occurrences of the command to "walk." This concentration of terms establishes unity in this section of the epistle. Therefore, all the seemingly isolated instructions or commands are linked to the broader command for Christians to "walk in a manner worthy of the calling to which you have been called" (cf. Eph. 4:1).

The Impact of the Vertical Relationship on the Horizontal Relationship

You are probably familiar with the breakdown of the book of Ephesians: chapters 1–3 (what God has done for us in Christ) and chapters 4–6 (how we live the life God has created for us in Christ). The division is sometimes referred to as the indicative and the imperative or the vertical and the horizontal or the theological and the practical. Some epistles are not divided quite so cleanly, but most epistles have sections of each. Preaching portions taken from either of these sections yield meaning in light of the interconnectivity of the two. The theological forms the basis for the practical, and the practical stems out of the theological.

A couple of well-known examples are the opening verses of Romans 12 and Ephesians 4. The "Therefore" in Romans 12:1 signals us to understand "the mercies of God" in light of the previous section. The same is true in Ephesians 4:1 where the, "Therefore," forces us back in the epistle in order to understand the meaning of "the calling with which you have been called."

While this connection between the theological and the practical is easy to recognize at the beginning of a section, it is easy to forget when we're several paragraphs into a section. For instance, if you're slugging away at some of the heavy, theological concepts found early in Paul's letters, it's easy to forget that a practical section follows. The theology does affect life even though our preaching portion may not contain any instructions for how LifePlus[24] operates.

Strings of Imperatives (Commands)

In your study of NT epistles you will encounter several impera-

---

24 I first heard this term from Dr. Douglas Green of Westminster Theological Seminary in Philadelphia. It is a helpful synonym for what is more commonly referred to as eternal life.

tives listed one after the other. Such strings of imperatives can be found in Romans 12:9–21; Galatians 6:1–10; Ephesians 4:25–32; Philippians 4:4–9; 1 Thessalonians 5:12–22; and Hebrews 13:1–17. The presence of a string of imperatives alerts us to a unique context.

When a preaching portion contains a list of imperatives, explore what relationship, if any, the imperatives have to each other. It's possible that all the commands have to do with a particular facet of living the Christian life. It's also possible that the commands are only loosely connected. That is, they are appropriate responses to a previous theological statement or broad statement about the Christian life (i.e., "walk in a manner worthy of the calling to which you have been called" in Ephesians 4:1).[25]

The command in Hebrews 13:4, "Let marriage be held in honor among all," finds its contextual meaning linked to either Hebrews 12:25 ("See that you do not refuse Him who is speaking") or 12:28 ("let us be grateful...and thus let us offer to God acceptable worship"). Obeying the instruction of 13:4 is a sign that the believer is not refusing Him who is speaking or a sign that the believer is showing gratitude, by which they might offer to God an acceptable service.

Here are a couple of examples of how meaning is fleshed out as we move from a textual big idea (texbi) to a contextual big idea (conbi) in preaching portions from the NT epistles.

---

25 Graves advises us that "Interpreting these lists requires determining whether the list in question is integral to the epistle's flow or is an aside on ethical behavior in general. Easton ... notes that one of the dangers with these lists is the fragmentary impression they might make on listeners. The items listed, though distinct, were intended to be heard as a unit, not so much as individual behaviors. The preacher needs to determine not only the meaning of the individual terms but also, and more importantly, the meaning of the terms considered as a unit." Cf. Mike Graves, *The Sermon as Symphony: Preaching the Literary Forms of the New Testament* (Valley Forge, Penn.: Judson Press, 1997), 182.

An example from Ephesians 4:25

> **Texbi:** The Ephesian Christians are to speak truth
> with their neighbors, because they are members of one
> another.

Concerning the flow of the argument, v. 25 begins with, "Therefore," which forces us back into the previous context. In vv. 22 and 24 the Ephesians are instructed to lay aside the old self and put on the new self. Also, note that v. 22 mentions their former manner of life. Further back in v. 17, we find instruction about not walking any longer like the Gentiles. This instruction is connected back to v. 1 that tells us how to walk ("in a manner worthy of the calling…").

What about the relationship between the vertical and the horizontal? Does the vertical relationship (i.e., the believer's standing or position before God through faith in Christ) impact the horizontal relationship (the believer's practice of their faith within the faith-family)? Chapter 2 tells us that the work of Christ has made all who are in Christ one new man that establishes peace (v. 15). Our imperative in 4:25 is a call to behave like we are one new man. We might also notice that the vertical section of Ephesians ends with an emphasis on Believers being rooted and grounded in love (cf. 3:17, 19). Our imperative in 4:25 shows love in action.

Finally, our preaching portion is found at the head of a string of ten imperatives. Even though these ten appear to be independent, they are connected to the concept of Christians walking in a manner worthy of their calling (vv. 4:1, 17). If I decided to preach the string of imperatives collectively, I might show the development of the idea like this: The Ephesian Christians are to walk in a manner worthy of their calling by speaking the truth.

When contextual meaning is factored in, the meaning of v. 25 can be expanded to: Christians continue to discard their old non-Christian ways and display the new person they have become in Christ by speaking truth with their faith-family members.

What does this expansion of meaning accomplish? It places the individual command to tell the truth in its proper context of a broader command to live the Christian life. The instruction to tell the truth is not simply a matter of being ethical; it's theological. All the instructions found in Ephesians 4–6 are what those who are "dead in...sins" (cf. 2:1) do when they are "raised...up with him..." (cf. 2:6).

The movement from textual big idea to contextual big idea helps guard the integrity of meaning. Notice that we have not lost sight of the meaning of the preaching portion. You can still trace the wording of the conbi back to the preaching portion. The conbi has traceability. But we have also honored the meaning of the immediate context. We recognize that the preaching portion continues to carry meaning that began in the previous context of the epistle.

Moving toward Canonical Interpretation

Some of you, because of hermeneutical and theological reasons, will be content to end the process now. You've seen a way to allow genre to communicate textual meaning and to allow the immediate context to potentially flesh out that meaning. You will enjoy the chapters that follow if one or more of the following are true: (1) Occasionally, your sermons contain connections to Christ; (2) You want to continue to think about the validity and effectiveness of Christocentric preaching; (3) You consistently practice a Christ-centered hermeneutic/homiletic.

6

CANONICAL INTERPRETATION: PREACHING ALL THREE CONTEXTS

"*Dale Allison is, I think, more accurate in saying of Matthew 1:1 that 'The interpretation of this line can be nothing other than the unfolding of what is not stated.' What is not there? Lots.... Interpretation is all about tracing out the crucial missing elements that make the text mean what it does*"[1]

"*...expository preaching can be too narrowly exegetical. It can*

1   Peter J. Leithart, *Deep Exegesis: The Mystery of Reading Scripture* (Waco, Tex.: Baylor University Press, 2009), 111–12.

*so focus on the immediately chosen text that we
fail to make clear how our passage fits into its
canonical context."[2]*

Our search for something to preach began with discovering the meaning of a preaching portion alone (texbi). Then, we fleshed out it's meaning in light of its immediate context (conbi). We found "crucial missing elements" in our preaching portion supplied by the context. That leaves one more context that often supplies additional missing elements—the context of the entire Canon of Scripture (canbi). This is what we want to preach; this is the bull's eye of our interpretation.

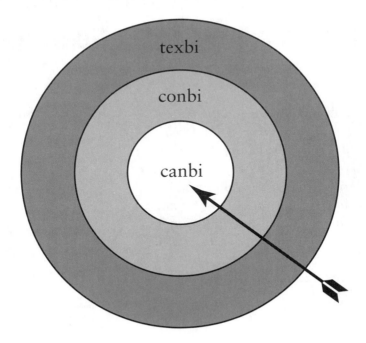

---

2   Ian Paul and David Wenham, eds., *Preaching the New Testament* (Downers Grove, Ill.: IVP Academic, 2013), 29–30.

Preaching with greater accuracy involves knowing what you're aiming at. Archery experts tell us that the smaller you make your target, the more accurate your shooting becomes—aim small, miss small:

> The outer ring of our target is the meaning, let's say, of Mark 1:12–13. The middle ring is what Mark 1:12–13 means in light of the context of Mark's Gospel. Our bull's eye is what Mark 1:12–13 means within the context of the entire Canon.[3] This is what we're aiming to preach.

In the following examples, notice what is missing if we do *not* interpret the preaching portions in light of the story of the entire Bible.

In Mark 7:14–23, after Jesus explains that sinful impulses from within defile us, He stops. We're left with no hope of being undefiled unless we can answer the question: How can a person become pure when all these sinful impulses defile us? Even though Mark 7:14–23 doesn't contain the answer, Scripture does and we need that information in order to accurately interpret Mark 7:14–23 in a way that functions for the Church.

A similar phenomenon occurs when preaching Proverbs 20:9. It reads, "Who can say, 'I have cleansed my heart, I am pure from my sin'?" I'm sure the correct response is, "No one can say that." I'm also sure the Canon contains another answer, an answer we need in order for Proverbs 20:9 to function for the Church. Our

---

3   Bock asks, "As the biblical theological context of a passage is deepened, how is the meaning of that passage affected?" Cf. Darrell L. Bock, "Evangelicals and the Use of the Old Testament in the New," *Bibliotheca Sacra* 142, no. 568 (1985): 309. Waltke defines canonical interpretation as "the recognition that the Text's intention became deeper and clearer as the parameters of the canon were expanded." Cf. John S. Feinberg and Paul D. Feinberg, *Tradition and Testament: Essays in Honor of Charles Lee Feinberg* (Chicago: Moody Press, 1981), 7.

sermon is enhanced when we show how God has made it possible for us to become spiritually clean.

When Psalm 119:9–16 is interpreted in isolation from the rest of the Canon, listeners are left trying to copy the Psalmist's feelings towards God's word. For instance, in v. 16 the Psalmist states: "I will delight in your statutes; I will not forget your word." Without consulting the rest of the Story, there is no way to know how a person can reproduce those same feelings for such a restrictive document. How does a person become like David?

I consistently practice a form of Christ-centered interpretation and application in order to fill in the gaps. At the outset, let me say that this approach is not focused on finding Jesus in these preaching portions. It's about explaining how each of these preaching portions makes complete sense only in light of what God-in-Christ-by-the-Spirit has accomplished.

For many years, I believed that when exegesis of my preaching portion was complete, my understanding was complete. McCartney and Clayton challenged my thinking by asking: "Does not any attempt to move from 'what it meant' to 'what it means' involve the whole Bible, as well as a changed situation, and will this not take us beyond what grammatical-historical exegesis can accomplish?"[4] My answer now is, "Yes, most of the time."[5] Here's why.

Either by explicit or implicit instruction, preaching portions in Scripture urge Believers to adjust their attitudes and actions.[6]

---

4   McCartney and Clayton, *Let the Reader Understand*, 159. Muller bluntly states: "Interpretation does not end with exegesis." Cf. Moisés Silva, ed. *Foundations of Contemporary Interpretation* (Grand Rapids, Mich.: Zondervan Pub. House, 1996), 541.

5   Leithart contends that Bible teachers "must spend their time unfolding what is not stated [in the preaching portion]." Cf. Leithart, *Deep Exegesis: The Mystery of Reading Scripture*, 112. Bracketed words added.

6   Implicit instruction occurs whenever biblical characters in a narrative give us examples to follow or avoid ("go and do likewise" or "go and do otherwise").

However, most of the time, preaching portions do not show how Believers can experience the desire and capacity to be or do what Scripture is calling them to be or do.[7] That means most preaching portions in Scripture need to be interpreted in light of the rest of the Canon.

Here is a pattern that I've observed over the years of listening to Tim Keller's sermons.

- The preaching portion describes or prescribes what Christians must be or do.
- The preacher explains why we can't be or do this in our own strength.
- The preaching portion directly or indirectly points to Christ who was or did what we could not do.
- The preaching explains how faith in Christ and the power of God's Spirit transforms us to be or do what the preaching portion describes or prescribes.

In one sense, this kind of preaching always arrives at the climax of God's Story as His Son becomes to Believers "wisdom from God, righteousness and sanctification and redemption" (1 Cor. 1:30). I find this pattern extremely helpful because, as you can see, it ends where it began—with application. The moralistic or transformational aspect of the preaching portion is not eclipsed by the rest of the Story. Arriving at the gospel is not the end; the gospel is the essential foundation for applying our lives to the Bible.[8]

---

7   My explanation for this is that God never intended for these preaching portions to stand alone. Although an expositor selects a section of Scripture to explain and apply, rarely is that section designed to be interpreted without foundational theology provided elsewhere in the Canon. The letter to the Ephesians was probably designed to be read and heard in one sitting. It is a complete letter in its entirely, but not when one paragraph is amputated and dissected on a Sunday morning.

8   This is an important distinction in this method. Of course, an added

This hermeneutic/homiletic requires a firm belief in the unity of the entire Bible. That belief blossoms into an approach that *consistently* allows the gospel to flesh out the meaning of preaching portions.[9] I emphasize consistently because many hermeneuts believe in the unity of the Bible, but do not consistently alter their exegesis accordingly. Exceptions may occur during the interpretation of messianic Psalms and prophecies. Many who believe in the unity of the Bible interpret most preaching portions in isolation from the rest of the Story.

Kaiser argues correctly that in order for biblical theology to function as "informing theology" for the Church, it must have a "canonical center."[10] A canonical center is an attempt to articulate a unified Story. Kaiser states his center as "...God's word of

---

bonus to this approach is that it avoids the prevalent tendency to urge listeners to respond to God's Word solely on the basis of their efforts. I'll say more on this later in a brief discussion of Bryan Chapell's brand of Christ-centered preaching.

9 Goldsworthy writes, "I am also convinced that the nature of the unity of the Bible is the key to biblical theology and vital to biblical interpretation.... Any kind of canonical approach presupposes a unity to the Bible that establishes the primary context from within which every text is interpreted." Cf. Graeme Goldsworthy, *Gospel-Centred Hermeneutics: Foundations and Principles of Evangelical Biblical Interpretation* (Downers Grove, Ill.: IVP Academic, 2006), 234, 46. Others, like Walter Kaiser, practice restricted theological analysis. While claiming to argue for "nothing less than a full involvement of biblical theology" as part of exegesis, Kaiser's method involves partial involvement until he is preaching from the book of Revelation. Cf. Walter C. Kaiser, *Toward an Exegetical Theology: Biblical Exegesis for Preaching and Teaching* (Grand Rapids, Mich.: Baker Book House, 1981), 137. On page 136 Kaiser exhorts expositors to compare the meaning of their selected Text "with similar... affirmations found in passages that have preceded in time the passage under study.... So serious are we about this point that we would prefer to rename this procedure the 'analogy of [antecedent] Scripture.'" On page 137 Kaiser states, "Surely most interpreters will see the wisdom and good sense in limiting our theological observations to conclusions drawn from the text being exegeted and from texts which precede it in time." Despite having profited greatly from much of Kaiser's thinking, I must respectfully disagree.

10 *Toward an Exegetical Theology: Biblical Exegesis for Preaching and Teaching*, 138.

*blessing...*or *promise...to be* Israel's God and to do something for Israel and *through them* something for *all the nations* on the face of the earth."[11]

Notice that this canonical center does not tell us how God's promised blessing came true or is in process of coming true.[12] Kaiser chose to leave out Scripture's portrayal of Jesus as the One through whom God's blessing would come to the Jew first and then to the Gentiles. I am suggesting that the gospel be inserted into one's canonical center. A gospel-centered, canonical center helps explain most preaching portions. As I showed above, leave this step out and you run the risk of under-interpreting God's Word.

The most common form of under-interpretation is some form of moralism. We urge congregants to be or do what the preaching portion is telling or showing us to be or do. Here's what this type of sermon sounds like:

- The preaching portion either tells or shows us what we must be or do.
- The preacher communicates the exegetical details of the preaching portion.
- The preacher exhorts the listeners to be or do this, and shows them appropriate steps to implement (the old "five ways to..." sermon).

Take a moment and compare this approach to Keller's approach discussed above. Under-interpretation occurs whenever I explain and apply a preaching portion without linking it to what God has done through Christ and His Spirit. Under-interpretation leaves out the

---

11 Ibid, 139.
12 This observation becomes an important part of my understanding of how Christ-centered preaching operates. It consistently fills in Kaiser's canonical center by showing how God-in-Christ brings His blessing to those who believe.

reason why God can command what He commands. God molds us
in light of how He made us.[13] Faith in the gospel leads to new ways
of being and doing.[14]

Canonical Interpretation:
What It Isn't and What It Is

Poor Origen is infamous for showing what responsible exegesis
should not do.[15] Canonical interpretation does not involve allegorizing that replaces the literal meaning of details in the Text with

---

13 Chapell advocates that sermons "incorporate the motivation and
     enablement inherent in a proper apprehension of the work of Christ..."
     Cf. Bryan Chapell, *Christ-Centered Preaching: Redeeming the Expository
     Sermon*, 2nd ed. (Grand Rapids, Mich.: Baker Academic, 2005), 12. A
     substantial number of scholars argue that the climax of God's Story is
     crucial for interpretation. Lischer states "...the preacher as theologian
     must discover how, in the words of Melanchthon, 'The Gospel opens the
     door to a correct understanding of the whole Bible.'" Cf. James Thompson,
     Preaching Like Paul: Homiletical Wisdom for Today, 1st ed. (Louisville,
     Ky.: Westminster John Knox Press, 2001), 125. Wright puts it this way:
     "the person and work of Jesus becomes the central hermeneutical key by
     which we, as Christians, articulate the overall significance of these texts in
     both Testaments. Christ provides the hermeneutical matrix for our reading
     of the whole Bible." Cf. Wright, *The Mission of God: Unlocking the Bible's
     Grand Narrative*, 31. Jensen states: "A good preacher will be a good biblical
     theologian. He will read the Bible as a book about Jesus." Phillip D. Jensen
     Grimmond and Paul, *The Archer and the Arrow: Preaching the Very Words
     of God* (Kingsford, NSW, Australia: Matthias Media, 2010), 83.
14 Kaiser's reaction to this approach is helpful: "Is the sole reason for
     preaching to bring the good news of salvation in every message? Is it not
     possible for preaching to address the believer and call for a response in
     light of the teaching of God's Word on ethics, morals, and an exemplary
     lifestyle?" Cf. Walter C. Kaiser, *Preaching and Teaching from the Old
     Testament: A Guide for the Church* (Grand Rapids, Mich.: Baker Academic,
     2003), 85. Notice that Kaiser does not link the gospel with the call for a
     response (or the application). I am arguing for a link between the gospel and
     application because of the way in which God links the two in the Old and
     New Testaments. I am also asking that we consider what our address to the
     listeners sounds like when separated from the gospel. More on that later.
15 I say, "poor Origen," because it's sad that he is known mostly for his
     excessive allegorizing. See Greidanus' section "Improper Ways of Bridging
     the Gap," in *The Modern Preacher and the Ancient Text*, 159–66.

deeper, hidden meaning. Our study of the preaching portion in its immediate context has yielded the meanings. We've attempted to show how those meanings fit together. At this stage of our study we do not need to go looking for more meaning in the details. It doesn't help our meaning to reinterpret Rahab's scarlet cord, for instance, in Joshua 2.[16]

However, in most preaching portions, we need to connect our selected preaching portion to the gospel. What this means is that Rahab's scarlet thread may or may not help us interpret Joshua 2 in the light of the gospel. If the thread is going to help us, it will function as a sign pointing to Christ so that His sacrifice fleshes out the meaning of Joshua 2. The gospel helps us understand God's saving act described in the narrative (the two spies being saved by Rahab, and Rahab and her household being saved by Israel). Having been brought from the Joshua narrative to Christ, we will be able to understand how Joshua's story means something for the Church.[17]

---

16 An excellent resource for reading how early theologians practiced atomistic interpretation is the multi-volume, *Ancient Christian Commentary on Scripture* published by IVP.

17 I believe that this is one way to put into practice the hermeneutic Jesus taught His disciples as recorded in Luke 24:27. For a more detailed explanation of this approach in contrast to the disconnected allegorizing of ancient theologians, see Randal Emery Pelton, "Creatively Moving to the Cross: Adopting the Goal While Adjusting the Method of Early Christian Preaching," *Journal of the Evangelical Homiletics Society* 12, no. 1 (2012). This approach helps us avoid the danger of Canonical interpretation overriding the literal, historical, grammatical, literary meaning. Commenting on the danger of reading too much canonical meaning into a preaching portion, Kuruvilla warns: "such a consideration [of contextual meaning] must not result in those individual voices [of a preaching portion] being 'outshouted by God,' thus denying the reality of the distinct utterances that compose the canon." Cf. Abraham Kuruvilla, "Text to Praxis: Hermeneutics and Homiletics in Dialogue" (University of Aberdeen, 2007), 126. So, in our example, the link to the gospel does not provide a different meaning conveyed through the storyline of Joshua 2. The gospel connection shows how the theology of Joshua 2 contributes to the saving and sanctifying of the Church. Poythress reminds us that "these extra things... are not somehow mystically hidden... so that someone with some esoteric key to interpretation could have

In his definition of *sensus plenior* (fuller meaning), Oss writes:

> The method does not consist of unbridled,
> imaginative eisegesis and the reading into a
> text of symbolic meaning that has no biblical
> basis. Further, it is not some sort of mystical or
> supernatural revelation acquired apart from the
> fruits of exegesis in which a previously hidden
> meaning is thrust into one's awareness.... this
> method is by no means to be separated from the
> grammatical-historical method and the human
> author's expressed meaning.... the two should
> complement one another as two aspects of a single,
> unified process of interpretation.[18]

The method outlined in this chapter shares this understanding of *sensus plenior* and attempts to anchor meaning to exegesis. Preaching with greater accuracy involves guarding the integrity and meaning of the preaching portion while also acknowledging that it means something within the larger biblical Story.[19]

---

come up with them just by reading... in isolation from the rest of the Bible.... Rather, the 'extra' understanding comes from the biblical canon itself, taken as a whole." Cf. G. K. Beale, ed. *The Right Doctrine from the Wrong Texts: Essays on the Use of the Old Testament in the New* (Grand Rapids, Mich.: Baker, 1994), 108. In Ramesh Richard's article, Packer puts it this way: "This [expanded meaning] is 'an extrapolation on the grammatico-historical plane,' not 'a new projection on to the plane of allegory." Cf. Ramesh P. Richard, "Methodological Proposals for Scripture Relevance, Part 2: Levels of Biblical Meaning," *Bibliotheca Sacra* 143, no. 570 (1986): 126.

18 Douglas A. Oss, "Canon as Context: The Function of Sensus Plenior in Evangelical Hermeneutics," *Grace Theological Journal* 9 (1988). For a helpful analysis of the concept and legitimacy of sensus plenior, see Kaiser, *Preaching and Teaching from the Old Testament: A Guide for the Church*, 193ff.

19 Vanhoozer writes, "My thesis is that the 'fuller meaning' of Scripture—the meaning associated with divine authorship—emerges only at the level of the whole canon." Cf. Kevin J. Vanhoozer, *Is There a Meaning in This Text?: The Bible, the Reader, and the Morality of Literary Knowledge* (Grand Rapids, Mich.: Zondervan, 1998), 264.

Before moving on, let me address a concern I hear pastors express frequently. Some are hesitant to employ this hermeneutic because of the fear of preaching redundant sermons. Will sermons sound the same if we always interpret preaching portions in light of the entire story of God-in-Christ-redeeming-His-world? The answer is "yes" and "no."

First, "yes." Every sermon sounds the same at the very end as we show that the preaching portion finds ultimate meaning in the gospel. Every narrative text that displays some slice of God's salvation or judgment is fully explained in Christ. Every law-like text that outlines how God's redeemed people live can be kept only in Christ. Every prophetic text that calls God's people to repent can only be heeded in Christ. It's the kind of redundant interpretation Jesus gave His disciples in Luke 24:27.[20] I love the venerable pas-

---

20 I have just given you some broad categories that can function as a guide to the kind of canonical interpretation I am advocating. I have these broad categories in mind during my sermon preparation each week. It gives me a place to begin the process of theological exegesis, exploring how the preaching portion functions for the Church. Chapell provides four redemptive foci that help us explore how the grace of God-in-Christ interprets any preaching portion. Cf. Chapell, *Christ-Centered Preaching: Redeeming the Expository Sermon*, 282. Now concerning Jesus' hermeneutic, debates rage concerning whether we can and should copy the hermeneutical methods of Jesus and His apostles. If we do not follow their interpretation and application of the OT, then how will we interpret and apply it and how will that interpretation and application function for the Church? Longenecker writes, "Our commitment as Christians is to the reproduction of the apostolic faith and doctrine, and not necessarily to the specific apostolic exegetical practices." Cf. Richard N. Longenecker, *Biblical Exegesis in the Apostolic Period* (Grand Rapids, Mich.: W. B. Eerdmans, 1999), 198. But can the two be separated? If our commitment is to the reproduction of apostolic faith and doctrine from OT preaching portions, can we do that without reproducing their exegetical practices? If we don't follow their practices, then what faith and doctrine will we arrive at from OT preaching portions that are not interpreted by the Apostles as recorded in the New Testament? Hays writes, "the Jesus who taught the disciples on the Emmaus road that *all* the scriptures bore witness to him continues to teach us to discover figural senses of Scripture that are not developed in the New Testament." Cf. Ellen F. Davis and Richard B. Hays, *The Art of Reading Scripture* (Grand Rapids, Mich.: Eerdmans, 2003), 234. Leithart sees this as a matter of discipleship: "I want

tor Criswell's reaction to Jesus' hermeneutic: "How could a man improve on that?"[21]

So, first, there is redundancy as each sermon concludes with a discussion of the cross. But, second, the answer is "no." Christ-centered sermons don't sound the same because most preaching portions have a uniqueness that prevents redundancy. The stories, laws, and prophecies display unique aspects of God's salvation. Each sermon will sound different until the gospel story is told. Each preaching portion leads us to the grace-of-God-in-Christ by different avenues.

Here are a few examples of how canonical interpretation affects interpretation. The examples represent large blocks of Scripture and provide general direction for many preaching portions.

1. Old Testament or New Testament narratives that describe God creating, saving, or judging His world have meaning ultimately when they are read in light of the Gospel.

What's missing in a sermon on the creation account of Genesis 1–2 that does not factor in the rest of the story? Well, in this case, practically everything is missing: the Fall and God working to redeem His people so they and all of creation can return to Eden-like existence in the new creation. Think about how a sermon on only Genesis 1–2 could function for the Church without the rest of the story. What could pastors do with that Genesis account alone? What's needed is an answer to this question: How can God's people experience life the way God originally intended it to be lived? The rest of Scripture provides the answer to that question.[22]

---

to read the Old Testament and the New as a disciple of Jesus, and that means following in the footsteps of the disciples' methods of reading." Cf. Leithart, *Deep Exegesis: The Mystery of Reading Scripture*, viii.

21 Feinberg and Feinberg, *Tradition and Testament: Essays in Honor of Charles Lee Feinberg*, 294.

22 Is this a form of eisegesis (reading meaning into Scripture) rather than exegesis (reading meaning from Scripture)? It may be fair to say that eisegesis

Enns likens the expansion of meaning to "the process of reading a good novel the first time and the second time. The two readings are not the same experience....the first reading of the Old Testament leaves you with hints, suggestions, trajectories, and so on, of how things will play out in the end, but it is not until you get to the end that you begin to see how the pieces fit together. And in that second reading, you also begin to see how parts of the story that seemed wholly unrelated at first now take on a much richer, deeper significance."[23]

Think of every Old Testament narrative in Joshua, Samuel, Kings, and Chronicles that shows God's people in battle. What determines whether or not God fights for His people is what kind of king they have. When the king honors God, God defeats the enemy. When the king dishonors God, God allows His people to be defeated. Readers could see that it was better to be under some kings than others.

What do these stories mean without the rest of the Story? The answer to the first question is most often: "Follow the example of the good kings (Josiah in 2 Chron. 34) and avoid the example of

---

of Scripture becomes exegesis of Scripture when the word "Scripture" expands beyond the preaching portion to include information from the entire Canon. In these examples I am reading into a preaching portion meaning that is found elsewhere in Scripture. In discussing how the New Testament writers understood the Old Testament, Enns writes, "the New Testament authors take the Old Testament out of *one* context, that of the original human author, and place it into *another* context, the one that represents the final goal to which Israel's story has been moving.... The reality of the risen Christ drove them to read the Old Testament in a new way [citing Matthew 2:15's use of Hosea 11:1 and 2 Corinthians 6:2's use of Isaiah 49:8]: 'Now that I see how it all ends, I can see how this part of the Old Testament, too, drives us forward.'" Cf. Peter Enns, *Inspiration and Incarnation: Evangelicals and the Problem of the Old Testament* (Grand Rapids, Mich.: Baker Academic, 2005), 153. Commenting on the way the apostles interpreted the Old Testament, Enns writes, "What constitutes a Christian reading of the Old Testament is that it proceeds to the second reading, the eschatological, christotelic reading—and this is precisely what the apostles model for us." Cf. *Inspiration and Incarnation*, 154.

23 *Inspiration and Incarnation*, 153.

the evil kings (Manasseh in 2 Chron. 33)." Sermons will outline the specifics of "go and do likewise" or "go and do otherwise."

When the rest of the Story is read, however, we see that the nation could not sustain a kingdom ruled by godly kings. Kings and subjects were not able to keep their end of the covenant.[24] Victory is not accomplished until our Perfect King arrives and conquers through seeming defeat on the cross. Everyone is urged to become a citizen of His kingdom. Anyone who enters God's kingdom through faith in Christ has the desire and capacity to emulate the good kings and avoid the example of evil kings.

2. Old Testament or New Testament didactic sections also contain meaning when read within the context of the gospel.

By faith in Christ, God's people have the desire and capacity to put His instructions into practice. I'm referring to Old Testament instruction given in the form of laws, sermons, and commands found within the larger, narrative context of the redemptive story. I'm also referring to New Testament teaching sections found within the Gospels and Acts and in the numerous letters.

What's missing in a sermon on Deuteronomy 6:4–5 (or Mark 12:28–32) if it's interpreted without the rest of the Canon? The preaching portion reads: "Hear, O Israel: The Lord our God, the Lord is one. You shall love the Lord your God with all your heart and with all your soul and with all your might." What's missing is how anyone is able to do this? I chose this preaching portion because it follows on the heels of God's explanation of the problem I've just raised. In Deuteronomy 5, after hearing all the commandments of God, the people ask Moses, "speak to us all that the Lord

---

24 I chose the route of "not able to" instead of "refused to" keep their end of the covenant because of God's assessment in Deuteronomy 5:29, a verse I refer to below. After acknowledging the people's good intentions, the Lord said: "Oh that they had such a mind as this always, to fear me and to keep all my commandments...." Refusal involved inability.

our God will speak to you, and we will hear and do it" (v. 27). They have great intentions and God even says, "They are right in all that they have spoken" (v. 28). Unfortunately God continues in verse 29: "Oh that they had such a mind as this always, to fear me and to keep all my commandments...."

The rest of the OT story tells us that they didn't have that kind of mind, but also how that mindset was made available. Jeremiah 31:31–34 and Ezekiel 36:25–27 tell of a future time when God's people will have such a mind. Romans 8:3–4 spells it out in slightly different language: "For what the Law could not do, weak as it was through the flesh, God did: sending His own Son... in order that the requirement of the Law might be fulfilled in us, who do not walk according to the flesh, but according to the Spirit." Here's how God transforms us into law-abiding citizens. What will the sermon sound like if it does not supply this data?

The same is true when interpreting New Testament didactic sections. Romans 12:21 reads: "Do not be overcome by evil, but overcome evil with good." Interpreted in isolation from the rest of Romans, I will explain what the instruction means and then urge faith-family members to put it into practice. I'll probably suggest extra-biblical principles explaining how to implement the instruction.

In many of the NT epistles, connecting the instruction with the rest of the Story means remembering the theological statements found earlier in Romans. Paul's instructions arise out of conviction that Christians can and must live a certain way. Romans 1:5 says, "through whom we have received grace and apostleship to bring about the obedience of faith...."[25]

---

25 You are no doubt aware of the sequence of many NT epistles: first, what God has done for us in Christ (vertical relationship between God and us; the doctrinal section) and second, how Christians respond to what God has done for us in Christ (horizontal relationship between us and our faith-family members; the practical section).

3. Several Old and New Testament narratives highlight the attitudes and actions of key characters.

Sermons will most often suggest that these narratives intend for us to either, "go and do likewise..." or "go and do otherwise," depending on whether the examples are good or bad. The narratives contain implied prescriptions within the descriptions. The displays of faith/disbelief or obedience/disobedience are teaching us how to live as Christians. The rest of the story, however, is needed to show us how we can follow (or not follow) the given example.

Take, for instance, the mini-narrative in Genesis that shows Joseph running out of Potiphar's house to escape the advances of Potiphar's wife. I doubt the story is designed to teach us how to avoid sexual temptation. I have no doubt the story implies that it is right to avoid sexual temptation like Joseph did.

Before we think about following Joseph's example, we might point out that salvation was provided through someone like Joseph. Why was Joseph's righteousness an important part of this narrative at this moment in history? Was it only to provide a moral example?

The desire and capacity to run away from sexual temptation is the result of trusting in Jesus who, like Joseph, did not do evil by sinning against God (cf. Genesis 39:9). We can preach the moral example once we have shown how Joseph's faith can be our faith too. So, it's not a question of whether we preach the exemplar or whether we preach Christ crucified. It's both/and.[26]

As I mentioned earlier, what do sermons sound like that do not interpret mini-narratives in light of the whole canonical Story? A few years ago a guest preacher preached from 2 Chronicles 34. The sermon listed seven ways King Josiah functioned as a catalyst

---

26 Concerning exemplars, Chapell writes: "This does not mean that biblical characters have no exemplary qualities for us to emulate (e.g., Rom. 15:4; Phil. 3:17). We must understand, though, that when these positive qualities appear, grace is the cause (Rom. 11:36)." Cf. Chapell, *Christ-Centered Preaching: Redeeming the Expository Sermon*, 303.

for God's glory. That same week I was running with a friend. His reaction to the sermon was both frightful and insightful.

He said the sermon made him feel guilty because it revealed how far short he was of reaching Josiah's level. The challenge to be like Josiah contained no hope for achieving the goal. The rest of the Story puts Josiah in a long line of kings who could not accomplish what only the King of Kings could accomplish. Salvation, including the ability to follow Josiah's example, is the result of faith in Christ.[27]

I've provided a few examples to show how canonical exegesis affects the interpretation of preaching portions. If there is any moving beyond the meaning of the preaching portion discovered through grammatical-historical-literary exegesis, it is simply showing how God makes it possible for us to be or do what the Text is calling us to be or do.

Theological exegesis supplies how God-in-Christ-by the Spirit accomplishes salvation and sanctification for those who believe. This is information that preaching portions alone often do not reveal. This canonical addition is my bull's eye.

One advantage of beginning with a textual idea (texbi), progressing to a context idea (conbi), and arriving at a canonical idea

---

27 Not everyone agrees with the need for this hermeneutic. My good friend, Ken Langely, urges homileticians and pastors, "Let's be sure that when we're preaching Jonah we really preach Jonah and not John; when we preach Ruth, let's preach Ruth, not Revelation." Cf. Ken Langley, "When Christ Replaces God at the Center of Preaching," in *Evangelical Homiletics Society* (Birmingham, Ala. 2008), 16–17. I counter with: Once the Canon was completed, was Jonah or Ruth meant to be preached alone? Kaiser says, "yes." He writes, "Old Testament texts yield Old Testament sermons!" Cf. Walter C. Kaiser, *The Majesty of God in the Old Testament: A Guide for Preaching and Teaching* (Grand Rapids, Mich.: Baker Academic, 2007), 17. But does the message of Ruth-alone differ from Ruth-in-Canon? What type of message does the Church hear when Jonah or Ruth are preached alone? Horton writes, "A noted pastor once told me, 'When I'm preaching through the Sermon on the Mount, I sound like a legalist; when I'm preaching through Galatians, I sound like an antinomian.'" Cf. Michael Horton, "Interpreting Scripture by Scripture," *Modern Reformation* 19, no. 4 (2010): 12. I am suggesting that canonical interpretation tempers such legalistic/antinomian meanings.

(canbi) is that the meaning is traceable. This method maintains a connection between exegesis and theology that functions for the Church. McCartney writes: "True *sensus plenior* is organically related to the historical meaning. That is, it should be a 'fuller' sense, not an entirely 'other' sense."[28]

This hermeneutical move has been compared to what happens when you read a novel or watch a movie the second time. Because you've seen the entire plot, some scenes take on a whole new level of meaning. There was no way we could realize the significance of that scene the first read or viewing. You didn't misinterpret the scene the first time around; the scene meant something in light of what was happening at that time in the novel or movie.

However, the scene contained more meaning when understood against the backdrop of the entire plot.[29] Green puts it this way:

---

28 McCartney and Clayton, *Let the Reader Understand: A Guide to Interpreting and Applying the Bible*, 164–65. Leithart agrees, "In this process, the original sense of the statement is not lost. It has to be retained to make sense of the fulfillment.... Similarly, when 'out of Egypt I called My Son' transfers from Hosea to Matthew, the original sense remains....The words have taken on a new meaning in this new setting, but a new meaning foreshadowed in Exodus and in Hosea.... That is, the meaning of the quotation is lost unless we see that Herod is acting like Pharaoh, killing Israelite children.... Matthew gives new meaning to Hosea, but the meaning he gives does not violate Hosea's original meaning. The meaning changes as Hosea's prediction comes to fulfillment, but the change is consistent with the original sense." Cf. Leithart, *Deep Exegesis: The Mystery of Reading Scripture*, 64–65. For a concise look at three views on whether meaning should be limited to what the human author intended, see Richard, "Methodological Proposals for Scripture Relevance, Part 2: Levels of Biblical Meaning," 124. A summary of four views regarding the use of the Old Testament in the New Testament can be found in I. Howard Marshall, Kevin J. Vanhoozer, and Stanley E. Porter, *Beyond the Bible: Moving from Scripture to Theology*, Acadia Studies in Bible and Theology (Grand Rapids, Mich.: Baker Academic, 2004), 48–54. One limitation of the discussion is that only prophetic passages of Old Testament Scripture are discussed. Much more discussion needs to take place concerning the interpretation of Old Testament narratives.

29 In his chapter "Uncovering a Second Narrative," Steinmetz writes, "once the second narrative is in place [i.e., what happened to Jesus], it is impossible to understand earlier events apart from it. In the order of being, the second narrative comes last. In the order of knowing, it comes first. That is why both mystery stories and the biblical documents are best understood by reading

"The first reading will also set trajectories that set the boundaries for the second reading. While the second reading can be creative and is based on redefinitions of key Old Testament concepts (and so is 'surprising'), it must still be 'true to the story,' that is, it must stay within boundaries set by the Old Testament's trajectories (the plural is important). So a grammatical-historical interpretation will set the parameters of the metanarrative, and establish provisional meanings.... Without first readings, second Christotelic readings are not true second readings and dissolve into allegory. And it is the redemptive-*historical* rootedness of my reinterpretation of the Old Testament that (I think) allows me to differentiate what I am doing from 'pure' allegory."[30]

The following image shows what happens as we move from the historical meaning of the human author to the theological/

---

the last chapter first." Cf. Davis and Hays, *The Art of Reading Scripture*, 64. Hays writes, "The puzzled Emmaus disciples have all the facts but lack the pattern, the integrative interpretation, that makes them meaningful.... The apostolic sermons exemplify the sort of readings that (we may suppose) Luke imagines Jesus to have offered on the Emmaus road." Cf. *The Art of Reading Scripture*, 230. In his analysis of Vos's approach, Doug Green writes, "I am suggesting... that Vos does not distinguish between the first reading of the Old Testament (a grammatical-historical reading, or a 'prospective reading'—reading towards an unknown ending) and a second reading (a Christocentric rereading in the light of the ending, that is a 'retrospective reading'). I think that Vos is actually performing a second (retrospective) reading under the guise of a first (prospective) reading. Perhaps it might be more accurate to say that he is performing a harmonized reading that does justice to neither the first nor the second reading and in so doing flattens the rough contours of the journey!" Cf. Douglas Green, "Introduction to Reading the Old Testament: The Redemptive-Historical Structure of the Bible," (Philadelphia, Penn.: Westminster Theological Seminary, 2005), 24. The method I'm proposing follows Green's preference for two readings. In my case, the first readings result in the texbi and conbi; the second reading yields the canbi.

30 Green, "Introduction to Reading the Old Testament: The Redemptive-Historical Structure of the Bible," 42–43. See also Paul Scott Wilson, *God Sense: Reading the Bible for Preaching* (Nashville: Abingdon Press, 2001), 112–36. A helpful discussion of a subdued form of allegory can be found in Graeme Goldsworthy, *Preaching the Whole Bible as Christian Scripture: The Application of Biblical Theology to Expository Preaching* (Grand Rapids, Mich.: W.B. Eerdmans, 2000), 76–80.

Christological meaning of the Divine Author. At the beginning of the interpretive process, we are heavy on the human side and light on the Divine side. At the end of the interpretative process, the situation has reversed. At either extreme, we never lose sight of the human (historical) or the Divine (theological). Really it is all Divine Authorial meaning and all human authorial meaning due to Scripture's dual authorship.[31]

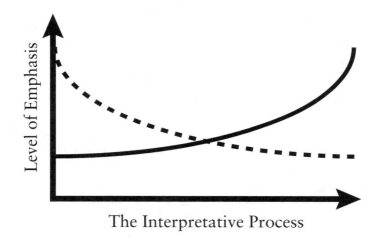

The Interpretative Process

■ ■ ■ ■ ■ ■ The Historical Meaning of the Human Author
▬▬▬▬▬▬▬ The Theological/Christological Meaning of the Divine Author

So, what do we end up with when multiple-author meaning is discovered? It should include a clear:

---

31 From another angle, it could be argued that more human authorship is encountered at the TBI level because we add, let's say, Paul's teaching to Moses. Divine authorship of the entire Bible results in multiple human authors contributing to the meaning of a given preaching portion.

1. Statement of what God has done for us through Christ, in the power of the Spirit. This begins to explain how the preaching portion saves those who believe (some facet of sanctification, but not excluding the justification of sinners who believe as a result of overhearing the interpretation).

2. Call to Believers and unbelievers to believe the gospel. Or, you might think of this as a statement of our confession that we do believe the gospel.[32]

3. Statement of how believing the gospel leads to the desire and capacity to apply life to the preaching portion. This creates a strong connection between our behavior and our salvation (sinful emotions and actions are the result of a lack of faith, while righteous attitudes and actions are faith-based).[33]

Before I show some ways to arrive at canonical meaning, let me allow Ferguson's exhortation to warn us. He writes, "These are gen-

---

32 This angle on interpretation sets us up to urge, or confirm, faith in Christ as the first phase of application.

33 Concerning the relationship between Christian living and the gospel, Goldsworthy writes: "One is unlikely to assert that we are justified by sanctification, but, whether done intentionally or not, that is what happens when we allow the teaching of Christian living, ethical imperatives, and exhortations to holiness to be separated from and to take the place of the clear statement of the gospel. We can preach our hearts out on texts about what we ought to be, what makes a mature church, or what the Holy Spirit wants to do in our lives, but if we do not constantly, in every sermon, show the link between the Spirit's work in us to Christ's work for us, we will distort the message and send people away with a natural theology of salvation by works. Preaching from the epistles demands of the preacher that the message of the document be taken as a whole even if only a selection of texts, or just one verse, is to be expounded." Cf. Goldsworthy, *Preaching the Whole Bible as Christian Scripture,* 237. In a sermon on the good Samaritan, Spurgeon said: "But let it never be forgotten that what the Law demands of us, the gospel produces in us. The Law tells us what we ought to be and it is one objective of the gospel to raise us to that condition." Cf. Charles Spurgeon, "The Good Samaritan," http://www.spurgeongems.org. This sermon is #1360 of volume 23.

eral principles; they do not constitute a simple formula, an elixir to be sprinkled on our sermons to transform them into the preaching of Christ. There is no formula that will do that. We never 'arrive' or 'have it cracked' when it comes to preaching Christ."[34]

I mostly agree. Ferguson's discussion of the general principles, however, overlaps with Greidanus' "ways" to Christ. So there appears to be the semblance of a formula, but not one that is airtight.[35] Ferguson also cites a "homiletical version of Thomas' five ways" to preaching Christ: (1) the preaching portion contains a direct prophecy about Christ, (2) shows why Christ is needed, (3) contains something that reminds us of Christ, (4) speaks of something that could not be accomplished without Christ or (5) shows us a person or people who are unlike Christ.[36]

These summaries provide possible pathways to connect preaching portions to the climax of the Canon. Let's look at how we can move from preaching portions to the rest of the Story.

Track Key Terms and Concepts throughout the Canon
Begin your search for canonical meaning by tracing key terms and concepts contained in your preaching portion throughout the rest of the Canon. Search in previous books of the Bible and in the books that follow. For example, 2 Kings 4:42–44 reads:

> A man came from Baal-shalishah, bringing the man
> of God bread of the firstfruits, twenty loaves of barley

---

34 Sinclair B. Ferguson, "Preaching Christ from the Old Testament," (2002), http://www.proctrust.org.uk/search/index.phphttp://www.proctrust.org.uk/product/articles-on-preaching/preaching-christ-from-old-testament-639. Cf. p.18.

35 Greidanus lists seven ways: (1) redemptive-historical progression, (2) promise-fulfillment, (3) typology, (4) analogy, (5) longitudinal themes, (6) New Testament references, (7) contrast. Cf. Sidney Greidanus, *Preaching Christ from the Old Testament: A Contemporary Hermeneutical Method* (Grand Rapids, Mich.: W.B. Eerdmans Pub., 1999).

36 Ferguson, "Preaching Christ from the Old Testament," 4–5.

and fresh ears of grain in his sack. And Elisha said, "Give to the men, that they may eat." But his servant said, "How can I set this before a hundred men?" So he repeated, "Give them to the men, that they may eat, for thus says the LORD, 'They shall eat and have some left.' " So he set it before them. And they ate and had some left, according to the word of the LORD.

If you were unfamiliar with the gospel accounts of Jesus feeding 5,000 men and 4,000 people, you might not connect 2 Kings 4:42–44 with Jesus' miracles. However, if you traced the term, loaves, or possibly, left (leftover), in the Canon, you would make the connection. You would notice that both stories deal with the concept of minimal amounts of food miraculously feeding huge crowds of people.

What does the Elisha story mean by itself? What does the story mean when interpreted in light of Jesus' miracles? Are those meanings the same? If not, how does the second meaning add to the first? Does the Church need the first meaning, the second meaning, or both meanings?

Certainly, the fact that "they ate and had some left, according to the word of the Lord" instills confidence in our God to provide for our needs. The story also provides a negative example. Baal-shalishah's unbelief in v. 43 urges us to go and do otherwise. The story also points ahead to Jesus. Ephrem the Syrian wrote, "[Elisha] prefigures him who multiplies twice some barley loaves and nourishes with them 'about five thousand men, besides women and children.' "[37]

However, simply showing that Jesus' miracles were echoes of Elisha's miracle doesn't affect meaning (or, the other way around: Elisha's miracles point forward to Jesus). We're not interested in the

---

37 Marco Conti Pilara and Gianluca, eds., *Ancient Christian Commentary on Scripture: 1–2 Kings, 1–2 Chronicles, Ezra, Nehemiah, Esther*, XV vols., vol. OT V, Ancient Christian Commentary on Scripture (Downers Grove, Ill.: InterVarsity, 2008), 165.

response: "Oh, that's interesting to see the similarities." If Elisha pre-figures Christ, how does that affect the meaning of 2 Kings 4?

What Elisha was doing for God's people, Jesus did even more. Jesus provided miraculous bread in the wilderness and became our Bread of Life on the cross. In this way God provides spiritual sustenance for those who believe. Our faith in the grace of God-in-Christ allows us to inhabit the world God's people were experiencing in 2 Kings 4, a world where God provides at all levels.[38]

Because God wrote one Story (not two stories or sixty-six stories) for one purpose, I expect to find repetition and restatement of key vocabulary. Vanhoozer cautions against what he calls "hyperactive reading... a frenetic allegorizing that finds associations never intended by the author...."[39] I'm advocating an interactive reading that allows other Scripture to influence the meaning of my preaching portion.[40]

---

38 Notice that expanded meaning takes place at the level of the entire plot, as opposed to a detail in the narrative. The bread may help us connect to Christ. That's a start. Ultimately, the gospel adds significance to the entire narrative, not just the bread. Salvation through Elisha points forward to the greater salvation accomplished through Christ. One of my criticisms of early Christian preachers is their tendency to make connections to Christ that are disconnected from the meaning of their preaching portion. Again, see Pelton, "Creatively Moving to the Cross: Adopting the Goal While Adjusting the Method of Early Christian Preaching."

39 Vanhoozer, *Is There a Meaning in This Text?: The Bible, the Reader, and the Morality of Literary Knowledge*, 397.

40 Leithart writes, "An interpreter not only has to know something outside the Text, but also has to know what information from outside the Text is relevant." Cf. Leithart, *Deep Exegesis: The Mystery of Reading Scripture*, 113–15. Leithart likens this process to what it takes to "get" a joke and why some don't "get it." The people who write jokes give no indication of the relevant information that is needed to "get it." Joke writers or creators of political comics found in the local newspaper assume that some readers will possess the external, relevant information necessary to "get" the joke. The problem I've witnessed in my own study of Scripture is that I know the external-to-the-preaching portion, relevant material, but don't always realize that it connects with the truth of the preaching portion. So, to use Leithart's analogy, when I practice only standard exegesis (without theological exegesis), it's like interpreting the joke solely on the basis of its wording, minus any pertinent, external information that makes the joke function as a joke. The punch line loses its punch without the external, contextual data.

Look for Quotes and Allusions in the Rest of the Canon

"The ore, it is true, lies half buried, but anyone who takes time to place alongside this text of Moses [Genesis 1–2] the words of the Holy Spirit in the New Testament will find great light, pleasure and joy."[41]

Because the Holy Spirit authored both Testaments, I expect key phrases to resurface from time to time as theological themes are fleshed out throughout redemptive history. This resurfacing can take the form of direct quotations and indirect allusions. An allusion is a veiled reference to an earlier concept. Remember, it's not sufficient to note that a direct quote or allusion exists. They must somehow contribute to the meaning of your preaching portion.

Mark 11:9 records the shouts of "those who went before and those who followed" Jesus: "Hosanna! Blessed is he who comes in the name of the Lord!" The quote comes from Psalm 118:25–26. What was said in the Psalm is now directed to Jesus as He approaches Jerusalem to rule-by-crucifixion. The cross is the ultimate display of God's "steadfast love [which] endures forever" (Ps. 118:1, 2, 3, 4). The scene in Jesus' life helps flesh out the meaning of Psalm 118.[42]

---

41 Wilhelm Vischer, *The Witness of the Old Testament to Christ* (London: Lutterworth, 1949), 51. Vischer was quoting Luther.

42 Realizing that Psalm 118 is quoted in Mark 11 also helps interpret Mark 11. Knowing what will happen in Jerusalem soon after His "triumphal entry," it is important to see a connection with Psalm 118:22 "The stone that the builders rejected has become the cornerstone." Mark 11:9 records the quote from Psalm 118:25–26. The meaning of Mark's scene is enhanced by much of the context surrounding verses 25–26. The context contains part of the story that the characters in the Gospel narrative have not yet grasped (i.e., that salvation from God would come through a crucified King). The same phenomenon occurs a bit earlier in Mark 11:2 where Jesus instructs two of His disciples to "find a colt tied." This is an allusion to Genesis 49:11. Part of the prophecy concerning Judah reads, "Binding his foal to the vine and his donkey's colt to the choice vine, he has washed his garments in wine and his vesture in the blood of grapes." This verse helps us understand what is happening to Jesus in Mark 11 as He approaches Jerusalem. Genesis

Here's another example from Psalm 22. Jesus recites some of this Psalm while He is dying on the cross for our sins (cf. Matthew 27:46). It's not enough for us to state this or to let our listeners know that Hebrews 2:12 quotes Psalm 22:22. Clowney writes, "David's Psalms and the other inspired songs of Israel carry forward the story of Jesus."[43] That's true, but we must go further. We must learn how the story of Jesus carries forward the meaning of the Psalm.

Clowney writes concerning Psalm 22, "on the cross, God the Father forsook the One who never forsook him."[44] That's true, but that's not enough. The question is how Christ being forsaken by the Father helps make Psalm 22 function for the Church. It's important to point out that because Jesus experienced this Psalm literally on the cross, Believers would never have to. God did forsake Jesus as He died on the cross for our sins. Now, all who are fully identified with Christ by faith never have to fear God's abandonment.

That's what I mean by expanding the meaning of Psalm 22 within the canonical context of the gospel. The expansion doesn't create a different meaning. Verse 19 says, "But you, O Lord, do not be far off! O you my help, come quickly to my aid!" We can count on our Lord

---

49:10 reads, "The scepter shall not depart from Judah...." Again, Jesus is entering the city of Jerusalem to reign, but His reign must include death by crucifixion. Although the characters in Mark's narrative don't realize who Jesus is and how His reign will be established, the Old Testament contexts make it clear. McCartney and Clayton explain: "If the NT quotes an OT Text, to understand what the NT writer is saying, we must go back and see what the OT passage was saying in its original context. This will usually clarify and elucidate what the NT writer is saying. Very often a NT writer will quote only a short excerpt from a passage in Scripture, expecting his readers to know the content of the entire passage.... looking at its larger context can still lead to valuable insights.... This principle also works the other way: if one is looking at an OT Text that is referred to in the NT, it is important to see how the NT writer used the passage; this will often indicate how the OT passage may be Christologically focused and ecclesiologically applied." Cf. McCartney and Clayton, *Let the Reader Understand*, 199–200.

43 Edmund P. Clowney, *The Unfolding Mystery: Discovering Christ in the Old Testament* (Phillipsburg, N.J.: P&R, 1988), 208.
44 *Preaching Christ in All of Scripture* (Wheaton, Ill.: Crossway, 2003), 189.

being with us because God was "far off" from Christ on the cross. Finding Jesus in Psalm 22 isn't important unless we explain how Jesus' experience affects our salvation in situations similar to David. I would argue it's impossible to give our congregant's hope without showing how the gospel makes Psalm 22 work for Believers.

Psalm 22

Old Testament		The Church
David *feels* forsaken by God; that God is far off; that God abandoned him.	Jesus *is* forsaken by God the Father, God *was* far off; God *did* abandon him.	Those who identify with Jesus will never experience God's abandoment.

Creatively Move to the Cross[45]

The vast majority of preaching portions require this final step of creatively moving to the cross. This is especially true in Old Testament narratives. These texts do not contain direct quotes or allusions. On a continuum, a quote is the clearest, most solid connec-

---

45 I am fully aware of the danger created by the presence of creativity in the hermeneutical/homiletical process. To be creative is to be inventive, imaginative. However, remember where we are at this stage of the method. Meaning has been developed within the immediate and intermediate contexts of the preaching portion. Creatively moving to the cross does not alter meaning, but clarifies how the gospel allows us to experience God's deliverance described in the preaching portion.

tion between two Texts and contexts. Next are the allusions—more indirect references. At the other end of the spectrum are, what I call, creative connections created by words or phrasing that takes me to some aspect of the gospel.[46]

Moving to the Cross

Effortless		Challenging
Old Testament Texts Quoted in the New Testament (Psalm 22)	Old Testament Texts That Contain Allusions (2 Kings 4:42–44)	Old Testament Texts That Require Creativity (Exodus 4:24–26)

This morning I was reading Exodus 31–34. which contains the story of God's people worshiping the golden calf. Part of God's judgment on His people was the order for the Levites to "kill his brother and his companion and his neighbor" (cf. Exod. 32:27).

---

46 Here's my reason why creative connections must be made in order to consistently utilize a theological hermeneutic. If Jesus displayed His hermeneutic to His disciples throughout the entire Old Testament—and I believe that is the best reading of Luke 24:27—then creatively moving to the cross was one of the ways Jesus interpreted all the Scriptures to them concerning Himself. If Jesus only displayed His hermeneutic in selected Texts, maybe He could get by with connections created through quotes and allusions. However, huge amounts of Old Testament material are not quoted or alluded to elsewhere. McCartney and Clayton raise this issue: "Since the NT writers do not cover everything in the OT, we may expect large areas where the typology or sensus plenior has not been indicated in the NT." See McCartney and Clayton, *Let the Reader Understand*, 167. Those large areas are either off limits to the Christ-centered hermeneut, or we can attempt creative connections. For an interesting understanding of Jesus' hermeneutic, see Matthew W. Bates, "Closed-Minded Hermeneutics? A Proposed Alternative Translation for Luke 24:45," *Journal of Biblical Literature* 129, no. 3 (2010): 537–57. Due to the time constraints of their walk, I believe Jesus moved systematically through the Old Testament and provided several examples to function as templates for understanding sections not covered. I would be interested in hearing your theories of how Jesus structured this key lecture.

In Exodus 32:29 Moses says, "Today you have been ordained for the service of the Lord, each one at the cost of his son and of his brother, so that he might bestow a blessing upon you this day." In v. 30 Moses goes on to say, "now I will go up to the Lord; perhaps I can make atonement for your sin."

One meaning or intention of the narrative is to urge Believers away from the kind of idolatry displayed at Sinai. In order to avoid this kind of sinful behavior, Christians need to realize how God-in-Christ has made atonement for their sin. The narrative provides a connection to the gospel by mentioning that the blessing of God could come upon God's people only "at the cost of his son" (v. 29). This is exactly how God provided atonement for our sin, including the sin of idolatry.

Another way to move from the Story to the Savior is in Exodus 32:30-35, where Moses pleads with God. Moses asks God to blot him out of God's Book if He will not forgive their sin. In verse 33 "But the Lord said to Moses, 'Whoever has sinned against me, I will blot out of my book.'" Thankfully, as you know, God did temporarily blot out One who did not sin against Him. God did not accept Moses' offer because Moses could not forgive sins through his own condemnation. However, God did accept Jesus' offer and Jesus' death-for-sin did stop the plague caused by our rebellion (cf. Exodus 32:35).[47]

---

47 Davis displays this creativity in her interpretation of Psalm 39. She writes, "the Gospel takes us deeper into this psalm....God must become one of the desperate. So in the fullness of time, God becomes a resident alien in the person of Jesus Christ." Davis makes this connection from the psalmist's statement in verse 12, "As for me, I am a sojourner with you, a resident alien, like all my ancestors." Cf. Davis and Hays, *The Art of Reading Scripture*, 303. On page 308–309, Hays moves to the cross from Daniel 3:25, the famous story of Daniel and his two friends being thrown into the furnace. Hays writes, "Did you notice, though, a strange thing.... The one whose appearance is like a son of God does not come out of the furnace of suffering. He is not miraculously preserved from the fire: he remains within it.... At the end of this story stands Jesus.... Jesus did not escape the clutches of his enemies; he did not emerge unscathed out of the furnace. No, he remained within it. He 'endured the cross, disregarding its shame,' precisely

Green writes, "There are times when the Jesus-ending does not have an obviously organic connection to Israel's story. There is something unexpected, surprising in this ending. Or to put it another way, rather than 'rolling' to Christ, sometimes, the Old Testament (or its grammatical-historical meaning) has to be 'dragged' almost kicking and screaming to Christ and brought into submission to him."[48]

Before preaching through a few OT historical books, I might have thought Green was exaggerating. Now I see more clearly what he is saying.[49] Again, at this stage of the process, bringing an Old Testament preaching portion into submission to Christ doesn't change the meaning of its theology. It completes the theology of the Old Testament by showing how God-in-Christ has accomplished salvation for those who believe.[50]

The way to connect preaching portions to the gospel is virtually endless. Maybe the best thing I can do for you is what a missionary friend did for me years ago: recommend listening to Tim Keller's preaching. If you listen to Tim regularly you will catch his

---

in order to deliver us to freedom and hope." Let me add that when Isaiah 43:2 reads, "When you walk through the fire, you will not be scorched, nor will the flame burn you," it's because the flames consumed our Lord on the cross as He suffered under the wrath of God.

48 Green, "Introduction to Reading the Old Testament: The Redemptive-Historical Structure of the Bible," 26–27.

49 This past Sunday I preached on Joshua 2, the Rahab narrative. In the discussion between Rahab and the two spies is the statement: "Our life for yours even to death!" (cf. Joshua 2:14). Rahab had confidence that God would save her because of this oath. We have a much greater confidence that God will continue to save us because of His oath described in Hebrews 6–7. I chose to connect Joshua's narrative to the gospel by saying that Jesus did exchange His life for ours on the cross. That transaction guarantees that all who believe in Him will indeed experience God's spiritual blessings, just as Rahab and her family did.

50 This is an important element of this brand of Christ-centered hermeneutic. In a minority of cases in the Old Testament the gospel does reinterpret. Because of the gospel, Christians do not engage in physical, holy war against enemy nations such as God's people did under Joshua's command. Christians do not stone adulterers. Most often, however, a Christocentric or Christotelic reading shows a connection between the Gospel and all of God's saving or judging acts in Scripture.

hermeneutic as he consistently finds ways to move from the Story to the Savior.[51]

The story of Jonah provides opportunities to see this creativity at work. Let me suggest a couple of ways to creatively move to the cross from Jonah chapter 4. First, in 4:2 Jonah tells God that he knew He was "slow to anger and abounding in steadfast love, and relenting from disaster." However, on the cross, God did not abandon His harsh intention to kill His Son to pay for our sin.[52]

Second, in 4:3 and 8 Jonah's words can be applied to Christ with new meaning: "...take my life from me, for it is better for me to die than to live." Jesus died as a result of this reasoning and this was the ultimate display of God's mercy.

Too far-fetched? These kinds of creative connections involve no risk. The meaning of Jonah is unchanged. The creative move to the

---

51 In an article entitled, *How to Read the Bible*, Wilkens describes our task of doing creative, canonical exegesis or theological exegesis: "The Bible becomes a vast field of interrelated words, all speaking about the same reality: the one God revealed in Christ, whose work was confirmed by the Holy Spirit in the life of the Church. The task of an interpreter is to help the faithful look beyond the surface, to highlight a word here, an image there, to find Christ unexpectedly, to drink at the bountiful spring whose water is ever fresh.... early Christian exegesis... was not about novelty but about finding the triune God in new and surprising places within the Scriptures." Cf. Robert Louis Wilken, "How to Read the Bible," *First Things* 181 (2008): 27. There is a fine line between novelty and creativity. While I appreciate and share a similar goal of early Christian interpreters and their pre-critical exegesis, I am suggesting a different kind of creativity. The creativity of much early Christian exegesis as displayed, for instance, in the Ancient Christian Commentary on Scripture, creates *essential* meaning. The creative relationship between isolated details of a preaching portion and Christ creates new and different meanings of preaching portions. The method I'm proposing creates *accessorial* meaning that can be traced back to the idea of the preaching portion.

52 I have found this angle fruitful for many preaching portions. The logic goes like this: God acts a certain way with Believers because He did *not* act that way with His Son on the cross. When Believers see God extending that kind of mercy to us at the expense of His Son, it changes us deeply and gives us the desire and capacity to be merciful (to be like God, unlike Jonah).

cross allows Believers to actualize the theology of Jonah by faith: "will you be merciful like the God who called you?"[53] This helps us avoid a moralistic, self-help interpretation/application. I can be merciful like God—unlike Jonah—only as my heart is warmed by God's mercy extended by a greater Prophet than Jonah. Believers don't follow Jonah's mercy-less attitude. They fight against selfish impulses by faith in Christ in the power of the Spirit.[54]

Comparing This Approach to Chapell and Greidanus

Because I encounter so much confusion about the nature of Christ-centered preaching, I want to end this section by showing how my nuanced method varies from the methods of two prominent homileticians, Bryan Chapell and Sidney Greidanus.[55]

Bryan Chapell

I refer to Chapell's approach as grace-centered instead of Christ-centered. Chapell writes, "The goal of the preacher is... to show how each text manifests God's grace in order to prepare and enable his people to embrace the hope provided by Christ." I propose that we follow up the display of grace in our preaching portion with mention of the primary display of God's grace in Christ.

Chapell reveals his method in his discussion of the Rahab story of Joshua 2. He writes, "Rahab does not represent the work of Christ because her cloth is blood red but because God demonstrates through her that he delivers the despicable (her) and the

---

53 Kuruvilla, "Text to Praxis: Hermeneutics and Homiletics in Dialogue," 91.

54 Can you see that Christotelic preaching is not an alternative to exemplar preaching? Christotelic preaching is one way to Christianize or un-moralize exemplar preaching. Again, it's not either/or, but both/and. I have no doubt that one possible meaning of Jonah is that he was intended as a bad example for Christians. However, I do not believe Jonah was intended to function as a bad example without pointing us to the perfect example of the Prophet who felt the same pity for the entire world that God felt for the Ninevites.

55 I have benefited greatly from the writings of both these men and am indebted to their work.

destitute (the Israelites) through means neither naturally possesses or deserves. In such ways, grace appears in Old Testament clothes and New Testament expression without direct mention of Jesus but with an unmistakable tracing of God's redemptive nature and work ultimately achieved through his Son."[56]

I agree with Chapell that Rahab's red cloth is not the best way to point to Christ. I prefer to show the connection between the grace displayed in the Rahab narrative and the gospel by highlighting that Christ eventually arrived through Rahab's family tree. One way Rahab points to Christ is that she joins the Israelites and marries into a very prominent family (cf. Matthew 1:5–6).[57]

Chapell acknowledges that sections of the Old Testament may be interpreted through the use of typology.[58] Acknowledging the presence of a legitimate type is a start. I suggest another step that connects the anti-type (the more fully expressed truth being typified) to the meaning contained in the preaching portion.

So, it's a start to announce that 1 Corinthians 10:4 teaches that the rock Moses struck twice in Numbers 20:8ff. was Christ. The question is how that identification affects the meaning of the Numbers 20 narrative: a call for God's people not to quarrel with Him about what He hasn't yet provided. This first reading doesn't contain the slightest hint that the rock was Christ.

The gift of water-from-the-rock was intended to bolster the faith of God's people. The miracle displayed God's ability to pro-

---

56 Chapell, *Christ-Centered Preaching: Redeeming the Expository Sermon*, 301.

57 I found it interesting that none of the ancient theologians included in Franke's volume connected the stories through Matthew's genealogy. Cf. John R. Franke, ed. *Ancient Christian Commentary on Scripture: Joshua, Judges, Ruth, 1-2 Samuel*, XV vols., vol. Old Testament IV (Downers Grove, Ill.: IVP, 2005), 7–15.

58 He defines typology as "the study of the correspondences between persons, events, and institutions that first appear in the Old Testament and preview, prepare, or more fully express New Testament salvation truths." Cf. Chapell, *Christ-Centered Preaching: Redeeming the Expository Sermon*, 281.

vide. At first glance, it appears that Paul's allegorization is a mean-ing changer. But let's look at what this interpretation actually does.

The Story now bolsters faith by highlighting God's provision of Christ. Christians who are satisfied with all that God is for us in Christ do not crave evil things and quarrel with Him. My wording comes from 1 Corinthians 10:6 ("Now these things took place as examples for us, that we might not desire evil as they did.").

The second reading is a true, second reading because we've allowed the first reading to communicate foundational meaning.[59] Then and only then can we move to meaning like: Christians do not crave evil things as long as Christ satisfies their thirst. God decided the Old Testament narrative functions for the Church ac-cording to this second reading.

Notice, only the rock has been redefined, not the plot. Accesso-rial meaning hasn't erased essential meaning.[60] And the intention

---

59 Speaking of John's use of Psalm 69 ("zeal for your house... has consumed me"), Hays writes, "Such retrospective reading neither denies nor invalidates the meaning that the Old Testament Text might have had in its original historical setting. Psalm 69 is fully comprehensible as an expression of Israelite piety: It is a prayer for deliverance in a time of trouble and suffering. When it is reread, however, in light of the New Testament's story of Jesus' passion and resurrection, it takes on additional resonances beyond those perceptible to its earlier readers. The figural correlation between the psalmist's prayer and the story of Jesus illuminates both in unexpected ways." Cf. Davis and Hays, *The Art of Reading Scripture*, 224.

60 Wright argues that the Old Testament already contains latent Christological meaning. He writes: "In the New Testament we reach the completion of all that God has accomplished in redemption. That does not mean a crude contrast in which we say, 'Previously God's redemption involved political liberation and social justice; but now we know it really means spiritual forgiveness.' Rather we see the totality of God's redemption in a way that now *includes* all that God has done—from the exodus to the cross. It is not that the New Testament *exchanges* a social message for a spiritual one but that it *extends* the Old Testament teaching to the deepest understanding of and the most radical and final answer to the spiritual dimension of our human predicament, which is already there in embryo in the exodus narrative.... What Israel needed was not just the ending of their exile but also the forgiveness of their sin. Both are contained in the prophets' vocabulary of salvation (e.g., Is. 43:25; Jer. 31:34; Ezek. 36:24–32). Cyrus as God's agent could take care of the first, but only the suffering Servant

of the original narrative remains: increased faith that doesn't quarrel with God. The Church is moved by the provision of Christ, a provision far greater than water-from-the-rock. Accessorial meaning has not transgressed the parameters set by Numbers 20:1–13.[61]

Sidney Greidanus

Greidanus is well-known for his seven ways to preach Christ from the Old Testament.[62] As I said earlier, finding a way to Christ is a start. Even though he moves from the preaching portion to Christ, his accessorial meaning will not necessarily connect to the specific situation of the narrative. What makes this especially difficult is that Greidanus is not a friend of exemplar preaching. This means you probably won't read him saying something like, "Follow Noah's example...." Inevitably, his meanings lean toward generalities, since the specifics of the narrative are dropped.

Greidanus proposes the following theme for preaching on Noah and the Flood (Genesis 6:9–8:22): Even as God judges the world for human sin and violence, in his grace he continues his kingdom on earth by making a new start with Noah, his family, and the ani-

---

of the Lord would accomplish the second. So the spiritual dimension of Israel's (and humanity's) need, and the spiritual dimension of God's ultimate redemptive goal, are both recognized within the Old Testament itself. The New Testament did not *add* a spiritual dimension to an otherwise materialistic Old Testament understanding of redemption. It tells the story of how God accomplished that deepest dimension in the climactic work of God. Nor is it the *replacement* of the Old by the New, but a recognition of where the Old Testament's insights eventually must lead if the fullness of God's redeeming purpose was to be realized." Cf. Wright, *The Mission of God: Unlocking the Bible's Grand Narrative*, 279, 85–86.

61 Speaking of his christological interpretation of the story of Daniel and his friends in the furnace, Hays writes, "the sermon illustrates the point that figural reading does not abolish the original historical reference of the text." Cf. Davis and Hays, *The Art of Reading Scripture*, 310.

62 Greidanus, *Preaching Christ from the Old Testament: A Contemporary Hermeneutical Method.*

mals with him.[63] Via typology, Greidanus' second reading yields: "in Christ God also makes a new start with his people...."[64]

Now it is important to show the connection between the flood narrative and the gospel of Christ. We could tell how God-in-Christ judged sin and extended grace to make a new start with Believers. How does God continue His kingdom? In Christ, God makes a new start with people who demonstrate their faith through radical obedience in a society filled with sin and sinners. Contra Greidanus, one purpose of the flood narrative is to present Noah as an example of faith.

Since Greidanus considers the particulars of the flood narrative inappropriate for preaching, he is left with a broad theme that bears little, or no resemblance to the original story. One of Greidanus' meanings for the flood story is: "God in Christ today still saves."[65] That is certainly true, but this meaning is untraceable. Greidanus has discarded the details of the flood. His new meaning could apply to several Old Testament narratives.

Examples of Canonical/Theological Exegesis
I want to present four examples of the results of canonical/theological exegesis. Although far from exhaustive, the genres I've chosen represent much of the Bible and may provide direction for tackling similar preaching portions. These examples show a way to incorporate canonical data to create accessorial meaning; they are not the only way. Notice what meaning is missing if this phase of exegesis is omitted.

Narrative Portraying God Saving or Judging
Genesis 11:1–9 records the story of God's reaction to the inhabitants of Shinar who attempted to make a name for themselves

---

63 *Preaching Christ from the Old Testament: A Contemporary Hermeneutical Method*, 321–22.
64 *Ibid.*, 323.
65 Ibid.

(v. 4). When the Lord saw the city and tower, He came down and "dispersed them from there over the face of all the earth, and they left off building the city" (v. 8).

Allen Ross states the following meaning: "If [Israel] was to survive as a nation, she must obey God's will, for the nation that bristles with pride and refuses to obey will be scattered.... God will subjugate the proud who rebel against his will."[66] Greidanus embellishes the idea: "The Lord scatters humankind, which in disobedience seeks to build its own, secular kingdom, in order to accomplish his plan that they 'fill the earth.'"[67]

The rest of the Canon shows God-in-Christ-by-the-Spirit reversing Babel at Pentecost (Acts 2) as different nationalities hear God's Word in their own language. Revelation 7:9–10 shows a great multitude from every nation worshiping before the throne and the Lamb. God's purpose in dispersing the people at Babel will be achieved. Finally, in order to avoid the fate of the Shinarians we must follow the one who, unlike the Shinarians "made Himself nothing" and "humbled himself by becoming obedient to the point of death, even death on a cross. Therefore God has… bestowed on him the name that is above every name, so that… every tongue confess that Jesus Christ is Lord…" (Phil. 2:7–9, 11). Faith in Christ creates Christians who obey God's will and do not bristle with pride.

Narratives Portraying Characters Doing Good or Evil

Second Samuel 11 records the story of David's sins surrounding his affair with Bathsheba. Kuruvilla suggests the following meaty meaning: "Unfaithfulness to God, the true sovereign, negates blessing and promises punishment with tragic consequences for individual, family, community, and society; such faithfulness as God

---

66 Allen P. Ross, *Creation and Blessing: A Guide to the Study and Exposition of the Book of Genesis* (Grand Rapids, Mich.: Baker Books, 1998), 243–44.

67 Sidney Greidanus, *Preaching Christ from Genesis: Foundations for Expository Sermons* (Grand Rapids, Mich.: Wm. B. Eerdmans, 2007), 125–26.

demands—perfectly modeled by Christ, the Son of David, the righteous King—embraces an utmost regard for the word of God and the reputation of God, and is manifested in the restriction of sensual desires and in the reined exercise of power."[68]

This meaning captures the general intention of the Story: to urge God's people to be unlike David. Notice that Kuruvilla has performed canonical exegesis by including Christ's example in his meaning. Believing that Jesus' example alone is insufficient to create Christians who can be more faithful than David, I want to progress from Christ's example to His atonement. Faith in Christ's sacrifice creates the desire and ability to not follow David's bad example of unfaithfulness.

Seeing Christ's example inspires us; believing in His sacrifice energizes us.

The narrative hints at Jesus' faithfulness. Unlike David, our King went out to battle for us (picking up on the wording of v. 1). Some might prefer to see the cross in the loyalty and plight of Uriah who was placed "in the forefront of the hardest fighting… that he may be struck down, and die" (v. 15).[69] In order for Christians to be able to demonstrate the faithfulness that David lacked, we must believe that Jesus' faithfulness has changed us to the core. Then we are energized by His Spirit to display a faithfulness God requires of His children.

---

68 Kuruvilla, "Text to Praxis: Hermeneutics and Homiletics in Dialogue," 198.
69 This pattern can be followed for numerous Old and New Testament narratives that function as exemplars (either positive or negative). Remember, you don't have to decide on preaching Christ or an example. We preach Christ so we can preach the example without moralizing. Take, for instance, Caleb's good example displayed in Numbers 13–14, and Joshua 14. The fact that Caleb "wholly followed the Lord" is a good example to emulate. Do we follow Caleb's example or do we connect with Christ, the ultimate Caleb? We do the latter so we can do the former. Only then do we have any hope of following Caleb's example as a Christian (as opposed to being a good moral person).

Psalms Expressing a Need for Deliverance

In many Psalms the gospel creates a bridge that allows the ancient prayers and praises to be ours. The first read of Psalm 3 might mean: In the midst of his enemies, David was confident in the Lord's protection and calls on Him for salvation. But, in order to function for the Church, the meaning morphs into: In the midst of our enemies we can be confident of our Lord's spiritual protection because Christ defeated Satan.

I must move beyond physical protection to the spiritual protection we have received through faith in Christ. I cannot say God will physically protect my congregants from any danger, but I can promise them on the basis of the gospel that no physical danger can keep them from experiencing LifePlus.

The Psalm contains allusions to what God-in-Christ has done. On the cross Jesus experienced the same taunting as David ("there is no salvation for him in God"; cf. Matt. 27:43 "He trusts in God; let God deliver him now"). Unlike David, when Jesus cried aloud to God, God did not answer Him from His holy hill (cf. Ps. 3:4). Or, you could mention that instead of David's enemies getting struck on the cheek, we read in Matt. 26:67 that our Savior was "struck" and "slapped." Either way, Believers are assured God saves them because of the cross.

Instructions on Living in God's Kingdom

This broad category includes Old and New Testament didactic material found throughout multiple genres. Matthew 17:24–27 could mean: Although exempt, Jesus and Peter display the humility of kingdom citizens and pay the two-drachma tax in order not to cause others to turn away from Jesus.

Information from the Canon might yield: those who trust in Christ relinquish their rights so that others might believe in Him. Faith in Christ fuels our obedience. Jesus commands His followers to show this kind of submission and humility because He knew His death-for-sin conquered pride and selfishness.

Conclusion

Canonical/Theological exegesis attempts to answer the following questions:

- How does the gospel make God's saving act recorded in the preaching portion possible for Believers?
- How does the gospel allow Believers to escape the judgment recorded in the preaching portion?
- How does the gospel provide the desire and capacity to put God's ways into practice as taught explicitly or implicitly in the preaching portion?
- How does the gospel extend the grace of God displayed in the preaching portion?

7

How Our Findings Contribute to the Sermon

I have introduced you to a method that helps you locate dominant meaning in your preaching portion. In my study, this usually takes place within the first couple of hours on Monday morning. At that stage of study, I'm far from having a sermon. However, I have made significant progress.

In order to show you how our findings contribute to the process of sermon development, I'll use two canonical big ideas from chapter 6. Here they are:

Mark 7:14–23 Human beings are defiled before a holy God by their sinful hearts, but Christ's death cleanses us.

Proverbs 20:9 Only in Christ can a person say, "I am clean from my sin."

Faith-First Application[1]

Our summary of the meaning of our preaching portion—the canonical big idea—contains latent application. This comes in two varieties, a general call to faith in the gospel and a more specific response often involving some change of attitude or action. The first form of application, urging faith in Christ, is rarely considered outside of the context of evangelism. I am talking about urging Believers to believe as the first phase of application.[2]

The presence of some element of the grace of God-in-Christ creates the platform for faith-first application. Having summarized the canonical meaning of the preaching portion, we now will ask our congregants to reaffirm their faith in the gospel. This is one response to the revelation of God; this is one act of worship. Urging Believers to believe is the first logical phase of application for gospel-centered interpretation. And we're going to ask them to do this before we ask them to apply their lives to the preaching portion.[3]

---

1   For a detailed look at—and justification of—the concept of faith-first application, see Jeffrey E. Carroll and Randal E. Pelton, "Cross-Eyed Application: Equipping Preachers to Urge Faith-Based, Text-Driven Obedience," *Preaching* 22, no. 6 (2007).

2   I am acknowledging two kinds of faith, the saving faith you possess and the sanctifying faith you exercise. The call to Believers to believe the gospel is a call to exercise faith that sanctifies. You might think of it as urging folks to exercise the faith they have in Christ. Apparently, Paul uses this sequence in Romans 6:11–12 "So you also must consider yourselves dead to sin and alive to God in Christ Jesus. Let not sin therefore reign...." First we consider, then we conquer.

3   The angle on application—applying our lives to the Bible, instead of the more familiar, applying the Bible to our lives—comes from Christopher Wright. Cf. Wright, *The Mission of God: Unlocking the Bible's Grand Narrative*, 534. Enns approaches the subject of application from the same direction. He writes, "The book of Exodus is not waiting there for *us* to bring it into *our* world. Rather, it is standing there defining what our world should look like and then inviting us to enter that world." Cf. Peter Enns, *Exodus*, The NIV Application Commentary (Grand Rapids, Mich.: Zondervan Publishing House, 2000), 31.

Notice how the sample ideas call for Believers to believe.

> **Mark 7:14–23** Human beings are defiled before a holy God by their sinful hearts, but Christ's death cleanses us. This sermon will show everyone how they can be undefiled through the sacrifice of Christ. One aspect of application will be to urge us all to reaffirm our faith in Christ's cleansing.
>
> **Proverbs 20:9** Only in Christ can a person say, "I am clean from my sin." Before we urge our congregants to be pure and clean, we'll ask them to reaffirm their trust in Christ's ability to cleanse them.

One benefit of faith-first application is that you will be ready to address every listener. As you appeal to Believers, you can also invite unbelievers to Christ.[4] Take, for example, an attempt to apply Ephesians 4:31, "Let all… anger… be put away from you…." A non-Christian may become aware that he violates this biblical instruction. He may even feel a desire to control his anger. Faith-first application keeps me from *only* giving him five ways to control his anger.

You know that the angry non-Christian has a deeper problem. Your canonical interpretation allows him to hear his need for Christ. Only then can the root problem be remedied. Cross-eyed application addresses his need to be reborn from above. What have I accomplished if I send him out trying to control his anger without faith in Christ?[5]

---

4   During the writing of this chapter, I finished reading some of M'Cheyne's Old Testament sermons. Near the end of his sermon on Zechariah 4, M'Cheyne has "A closing word to Christ's people, and to unbelievers: Be not faithless, but believing…." Both sets of hearers are addressed with the same application. Cf. Michael D. McMullen, ed. *Robert Murray M'cheyne: Old Testament Sermons* (Edinburgh: Banner of Truth Trust, 2004), 166.

5   Of course, I don't want to send my Christian listeners out thinking they can achieve practical righteousness apart from faith, either. So, both Christian and non-Christian are challenged to apply their lives to the Bible on the

Establish the Purpose of Your Sermon

The purpose of a sermon explains what God wants us to do as a result of hearing His Word. Any attempts during the sermon to apply our lives to the Bible involve fulfilling this purpose. We want purpose to flow directly out of the dominant idea we've discovered in the preaching portion. There may be other roads to application, but let's start with the primary purpose derived from the primary idea. Look, again, at the following two ideas:

> **Mark 7:14–23** Human beings are defiled before a holy God by their sinful hearts, but Christ's death cleanses us. Upon hearing this message, God intends for all His people to live undefiled lives. This includes avoiding the list of sins in verses 21–22.

> **Proverbs 20:9** Only in Christ can a person say, "I am clean from my sin." Although this proverb doesn't offer specifics, the sermon will urge all Christians to continue to confess, repent, and replace sins with righteousness.

I am a firm believer in thinking about application early in the sermon development process. Like me, you may have been cautioned about allowing thoughts of application to creep into your exegesis. The verb, creep, says a lot. But, the method we've been working

---

foundation of faith in Christ. Readers who are interested in, experimenting with, or fully engaged in a seeker-sensitive approach to preaching should sense the applicability of cross-eyed application for their audiences. You are trying to reach non-Christians with messages that are relevant to their lives. Putting away anger is certainly relevant to many lives, but the call of Scripture is not simply to put away anger for the sake of personal and relational health. God is calling every hearer of Ephesians 4:31 to put away anger because this type of anger is a mark of unbelief in the work of Christ, an unbelief that has eternal consequences.

through protects the integrity of interpretation. So, early in the week I want to know what the preaching portion is designed to do to us listeners. I don't want to wait until the end of the week to figure out how worship will result from the communication of theology.[6] I want to know the trajectory of the sermon as early as possible.

How You Will Introduce Your Sermon

I often think through sermon introductions late in the week. However, my canonical big idea does provide direction for the introduction. I will choose between introducing only the subject of the big idea or the entire big idea.[7] Here's how an inductive approach determines what is introduced.

Mark 7:14–23 Human beings are defiled before a holy God by their sinful hearts, but Christ's death cleanses us. You will want to introduce the idea of human beings being defiled in the eyes of God.

Proverbs 20:9 Only in Christ can a person say, "I am clean from my sin." You will introduce the concept of people claiming to be clean from their sin and guilt. In this way, the subject of your introduction matches the subject of your sermon.

Creating Need in the Introduction

I try to make sure my introductions show why we need to hear this

---

6 I understand worship to be the Believer's response to the revelation of God in a particular preaching portion.

7 If you are fond of deductive preaching, then you will want to introduce the entire idea and allow the sermon to break it down. If you enjoy inductive preaching, you will most likely introduce the subject of the idea and allow the sermon to complete it as the sermon progresses.

sermon. It allows application and relevance to occur in the first few minutes of the sermon. Before I ask us all to turn to the preaching portion, I want to tell them why we need to. Note the following:

Mark 7:14–23 Human beings are defiled before a holy God by their sinful hearts, but Christ's death cleanses us. Before turning to the Text, I want us all to know that we need to be cleansed in order to enjoy life with a holy God. We all need clean hearts.

Proverbs 20:9 Only in Christ can a person say, "I am clean from my sin." Again, I want everyone to hear how important it is that we are clean from all sin before a holy God. In the introduction, I'll introduce the subject of our inability to claim sinlessness or guiltlessness. Then, I'll announce that we need this in order to answer to a holy God.

CONCLUSION

OK. It's late Monday morning. You've put in a few hours of study for the Sunday sermon. You've selected your preaching portion. You're confident it has enough independence to preach a theological concept in context. You understand how all the various sized ideas fit together to communicate theology for the Church. In these few hours you have the seeds of sermon application and introduction. Basically, you know how this preaching portion functions for the Church.

Now, you can devote time to your exegesis and exposition of the preaching portion. Having the big picture of meaning provides hooks upon which to hang all the data you'll amass throughout the rest of the week. All along the way, you'll be double-checking your results. You may have to tweak some things. You'll be crafting your words and illustrating as needed. You'll be internalizing the message all week long so that, Lord willing, on Sunday, you'll be able to say to your faith-family: "Let me tell you what God is saying to us this morning."

BIBLIOGRAPHY

Alter, Robert. *The Art of Biblical Narrative*. New York, N.Y.: Basic Books, 1981.

Barth, Karl. *Homiletics*. Louisville, Ky.: Westminster/John Knox, 1991.

Bates, Matthew W. "Closed-Minded Hermeneutics? A Proposed Alternative Translation for Luke 24:45." *Journal of Biblical Literature* 129, no. 3 (2010): 537–57.

Beale, G. K., ed. *The Right Doctrine from the Wrong Texts: Essays on the Use of the Old Testament in the New*. Grand Rapids, Mich.: Baker, 1994.

Bell, Rob. "The Subversive Art." http://ctlibrary.com/le/2004/spring/1.24.

Bock, Darrell L. "Evangelicals and the Use of the Old Testament in the New." *Bibliotheca Sacra* 142, no. 568 (10, 1985): 306–19.

Bruce, F. F. *1 and 2 Corinthians*. New Century Bible. London, England: Oliphants, 1971.

Carson, D. A. "The Tabula Rasa Fallacy: Why We Must Become Self-Conscious about Our Interpretation." *Modern Reformation* 8, no. 4 (1999): 29–32, 43.

Chapell, Bryan. *Christ-Centered Preaching: Redeeming the Expository Sermon*. 2nd ed. Grand Rapids, Mich.: Baker Academic, 2005.

Chisholm, Robert B. *From Exegesis to Exposition: A Practical Guide to Using Biblical Hebrew*. Grand Rapids, Mich.: Baker Books, 1998.

Clowney, Edmund P. *Preaching and Biblical Theology*. Grand Rapids, Mich.: Eerdmans, 1961.

_____. *Preaching Christ in All of Scripture*. Wheaton, Ill.: Crossway, 2003.

_____. *The Unfolding Mystery: Discovering Christ in the Old Testament.* Phillipsburg, N.J.: P&R, 1988.

Conzelmann, Hans. *1 Corinthians: A Commentary on the First Epistle to the Corinthians.* Hermeneia—a Critical and Historical Commentary on the Bible. Philadelphia, Penn.: Fortress Press, 1975.

Davis, Dale Ralph. *The Word Became Fresh: How to Preach from Old Testament Narrative Texts.* Fearn, Ross-shire, Scotland: Christian Focus, 2006.

Davis, Ellen F., and Richard B. Hays. *The Art of Reading Scripture* [in English]. Grand Rapids, Mich.: Eerdmans, 2003.

Enns, Peter. *Exodus.* The NIV Application Commentary. Grand Rapids, Mich.: Zondervan Publishing House, 2000.

_____. *Inspiration and Incarnation: Evangelicals and the Problem of the Old Testament.* Grand Rapids, Mich.: Baker Academic, 2005.

Feinberg, John S., and Paul D. Feinberg. *Tradition and Testament: Essays in Honor of Charles Lee Feinberg.* Chicago, Ill.: Moody Press, 1981.

Fee, Gordon D., and Douglas K. Stuart. *How to Read the Bible for All Its Worth: A Guide to Understanding the Bible.* Grand Rapids, Mich.: Zondervan, 1982.

Fee, Gordon D. *New Testament Exegesis: A Handbook for Students and Pastors.* 3rd ed. Louisville, Ky.: Westminster John Knox Press, 2002.

Ferguson, Sinclair B. "Preaching Christ from the Old Testament." (2002). http://www.proctrust.org.uk/search/index.ph

Fowl, Stephen E. *Engaging Scripture: A Model for Theological Interpretation.* 1. publ. ed. Oxford: Blackwell, 1998.

Franke, John R., ed. *Ancient Christian Commentary on Scripture: Joshua, Judges, Ruth, 1-2 Samuel.* edited by Thomas C. Oden. XV vols. Vol. Old Testament IV. Downers Grove, Ill.: IVP, 2005.

Gaebelein, Frank, ed. *The Expositor's Bible Commentary.* 12 vols. Vol. 10. Grand Rapids, Mich.: Zondervan Pub. House, 1976.

Goldingay, John. "That You May Know That Yahweh Is God: A Study in the Relationship between Theology and Historical Truth in the Old Testament." *Tyndale Bulletin* 23 (1972): 58–93.

Goldsworthy, Graeme. *Gospel-Centred Hermeneutics: Foundations and Principles of Evangelical Biblical Interpretation.* Downers Grove, Ill.: IVP Academic, 2006.

_____. *Preaching the Whole Bible as Christian Scripture: The Application of Biblical Theology to Expository Preaching.* Grand Rapids, Mich.: W.B. Eerdmans, 2000.

Graves, Mike. *The Sermon as Symphony: Preaching the Literary Forms of the New Testament*. Valley Forge, Penn.: Judson, 1997.

Green, Douglas. "Introduction to Reading the Old Testament: The Redemptive-Historical Structure of the Bible." Philadelphia, Penn.: Westminster Theological Seminary, 2005.

Greidanus, Sidney. *The Modern Preacher and the Ancient Text: Interpreting and Preaching Biblical Literature*. Grand Rapids, Mich.: Eerdmans, 1988.

_____. *Preaching Christ from Genesis: Foundations for Expository Sermons*. Grand Rapids, Mich.: William B. Eerdmans, 2007.

_____. *Preaching Christ from the Old Testament: A Contemporary Hermeneutical Method*. Grand Rapids, Mich.: W.B. Eerdmans Pub., 1999.

Grimmond, Phillip D. Jensen, and Paul. *The Archer and the Arrow: Preaching the Very Words of God*. Kingsford, NSW, Australia: Matthias Media, 2010.

Guinness, Os. *Prophetic Untimeliness: A Challenge to the Idol of Relevance*. Grand Rapids, Mich.: Baker Books, 2003.

Hawkins, Greg L., and Cally Parkinson. *Reveal: Where Are You?* Barrington, Ill.: Willow Creek Resources, 2007.

Haynes, Stephen R., and Steven L. McKenzie, eds. *To Each Its Own Meaning: An Introduction to Biblical Criticisms and Their Applications*. Rev. and expanded. ed. Louisville, Ky.: Westminster John Knox Press, 1999.

Hendricks, Howard G., and William Hendricks. *Living by the Book*. Chicago, Ill.: Moody Press, 1991.

Horton, Michael. "Free Space: Interviews from Our Archives." *Modern Reformation* 11, no. 1 (2002): 33–34.

_____. "Interpreting Scripture by Scripture." *Modern Reformation* 19, no. 4 (2010): 10–15.

Johnson, Dennis E. *Him We Proclaim: Preaching Christ from All the Scriptures*. 1st ed. Phillipsburg, N.J.: P&R Pub., 2007.

Kaiser, Walter C. *The Majesty of God in the Old Testament: A Guide for Preaching and Teaching*. Grand Rapids, Mich.: Baker Academic, 2007.

_____. *Preaching and Teaching from the Old Testament: A Guide for the Church*. Grand Rapids, Mich.: Baker Academic, 2003.

_____. *Toward an Exegetical Theology: Biblical Exegesis for Preaching and Teaching*. Grand Rapids, Mich.: Baker Book House, 1981.

Kuruvilla, Abraham. *Privilege the Text!: A Theological Hermeneutic for Preaching*. Chicago, Ill.: Moody, 2013.

_____. "Text to Praxis: Hermeneutics and Homiletics in Dialogue." University of Aberdeen, 2007.

Langley, Ken. "When Christ Replaces God at the Center of Preaching." In Evangelical Homiletics Society. Birmingham, Ala., 2008.

Leithart, Peter J. *Deep Exegesis: The Mystery of Reading Scripture*. Waco, Tex.: Baylor University Press, 2009.

Lloyd-Jones, D. Martyn. *Preaching & Preachers*. 40th Anniversary Edition ed. Grand Rapids, Mich.: Zondervan, 2011.

Longenecker, Richard N. *Biblical Exegesis in the Apostolic Period*. Grand Rapids, Mich.: W. B. Eerdmans, 1999.

Longman, Tremper. *Proverbs* [in English]. Baker Commentary on the Old Testament Wisdom and Psalms. Grand Rapids, Mich.: Baker Academic, 2006.

Luther, Martin. *The Complete Sermons of Martin Luther*. 7 vols. Vol. 6, Grand Rapids, Mich.: Baker, 2000.

MacArthur, John. *Rediscovering Expository Preaching*. Dallas, Tex.: Word, 1992.

Marshall, I. Howard, Kevin J. Vanhoozer, and Stanley E. Porter. *Beyond the Bible: Moving from Scripture to Theology. Acadia Studies in Bible and Theology*. Grand Rapids, Mich.: Baker Academic, 2004.

McCartney, Dan, and Charles Clayton. *Let the Reader Understand: A Guide to Interpreting and Applying the Bible*. 2nd ed. Phillipsburg, N.J.: P&R Pub., 2002.

McMullen, Michael D., ed. *Robert Murray M'cheyene: Old Testament Sermons*. Edinburgh: Banner of Truth Trust, 2004.

Olasky, Marvin. "'It All Fit Together': Interview with Bill Moyer." *World* 23, no. 5 (2009): 23–25.

Osborne, Grant R. *The Hermeneutical Spiral: A Comprehensive Introduction to Biblical Interpretation*. Downers Grove, Ill.: InterVarsity Press, 1991.

Oss, Douglas A. "Canon as Context: The Function of Sensus Plenior in Evangelical Hermeneutics." *Grace Theological Journal* 9 (Spr 1988): 105–27.

Paul, Ian, and David Wenham, eds. *Preaching the New Testament*. Downers Grove, Ill.: IVP Academic, 2013.

Pelton, Randal Emery. "Creatively Moving to the Cross: Adopting the Goal While Adjusting the Method of Early Christian Preaching." *Journal of the Evangelical Homiletics Society* 12, no. 1 (2012): 4–15.

Pelton, Jeffrey E. Carroll and Randal E. "Cross-Eyed Application: Equipping Preachers to Urge Faith-Based, Text-Driven Obedience." *Preaching* 22, no. 6 (May/June 2007): 6–12.

Pilara, Marco Conti, and Gianluca, eds. *Ancient Christian Commentary on Scripture: 1–2 Kings, 1–2 Chronicles, Ezra, Nehemiah, Esther.* edited by Thomas C. Oden. XV vols. Vol. OT V, Ancient Christian Commentary on Scripture. Downers Grove, Ill.: InterVarsity, 2008.

Pratt, Richard L. *He Gave Us Stories.* Phillipsburg, N.J.: P. & R. Pub., 1993.

Quicke, Michael J. *360-Degree Preaching: Hearing, Speaking, and Living the Word.* Grand Rapids, Mich.: Baker Academic, 2003.

Radford, Shawn D. "The New Homiletic within Non-Christendom." *JEHS* 5 (2005): 4–18.

Richard, Ramesh P. "Methodological Proposals for Scripture Relevance, Part 2: Levels of Biblical Meaning." *Bibliotheca Sacra* 143, no. 570 (04 1986): 123–33.

Robinson, Haddon W. *Biblical Preaching: The Development and Delivery of Expository Messages.* 2nd ed. Grand Rapids, Mich.: Baker Academic, 2001.

Ross, Allen P. *Creation and Blessing: A Guide to the Study and Exposition of the Book of Genesis.* Grand Rapids, Mich.: Baker Books, 1998.

Ryken, Leland. *How to Read the Bible as Literature.* Grand Rapids, Mich.: Academie Books, 1984.

Ryken, Leland, and Jim Wilhoit. *Effective Bible Teaching.* Grand Rapids, Mich.: Baker, 1988.

Silva, Moisés, ed. *Foundations of Contemporary Interpretation.* Grand Rapids, Mich.: Zondervan Pub. House, 1996.

Spurgeon, Charles. "The Good Samaritan." http://www.spurgeongems.org.

Stott, John R. W. *Between Two Worlds: The Art of Preaching in the Twentieth Century.* 1st American ed. Grand Rapids, Mich.: W.B. Eerdmans, 1982.

Sunukjian, Donald R. *Invitation to Biblical Preaching: Proclaiming Truth with Clarity and Revelance.* Invitation to Theological Studies Series ; 2. Grand Rapids, Mich.: Kregel Publications, 2007.

Thompson, James. *Preaching Like Paul: Homiletical Wisdom for Today.* 1st ed. Louisville, Ky.: Westminster John Knox Press, 2001.

Tornfelt, John V. "Preaching the Psalms: Understanding the Chiastic Structures for Greater Clarity." *Evangelical Homiletics Society* 2, no. 2 (2002): 4–31.

Vanhoozer, Kevin J. *Is There a Meaning in This Text?: The Bible, the Reader, and the Morality of Literary Knowledge*. Grand Rapids, Mich.: Zondervan, 1998.

Vischer, Wilhelm. *The Witness of the Old Testament to Christ*. London: Lutterworth, 1949.

Waltke, Bruce K. *The Book of Proverbs: Chapters 1–15*. The New International Commentary on the Old Testament. Grand Rapids, Mich.: Eerdmans, 2004.

Warren, Rick. *The Purpose-Driven Church*. Grand Rapids, Mich.: Zondervan Pub., 1995.

Westphal, Merold. *Whose Community? Which Interpretation? Philosophical Hermeneutics for the Church*. The Church and Postmodern Culture. edited by James K. A. Smith Grand Rapids, Mich.: Baker Academic, 2009.

_____. *Whose Community? Which Interpretation? The Church and Postmodern Culture*. edited by James K. A. Smith Grand Rapids, Mich: Baker Academic, 2009.

Wilken, Robert Louis. "How to Read the Bible." *First Things* 181 (2008): 24–27.

Wilson, Paul Scott. *God Sense: Reading the Bible for Preaching*. Nashville: Abingdon Press, 2001.

_____. *Preaching and Homiletical Theory*. Preaching and Its Partners. St. Louis, Mo.: Chalice Press, 2004.

Wright, Christopher J. H. *The Mission of God: Unlocking the Bible's Grand Narrative*. Downers Grove, Ill: IVP Academic, 2006.